Henry VIII's Last Love

Henry VIII's Last Love

The Extraordinary Life of Katherine Willoughby, Lady-in-Waiting to the Tudors

David Baldwin

AMBERLEY

First published 2015

Amberley Publishing
The Hill, Stroud
Gloucestershire, GL5 4EP

www.amberley-books.com

Copyright © David Baldwin, 2015

The right of David Baldwin to be identified as
the Author of this work has been asserted in
accordance with the Copyrights, Designs and
Patents Act 1988.

ISBN 978 1 4456 4104 1 (hardback)
ISBN 978 1 4456 4113 3 (ebook)

British Library Cataloguing in Publication Data.
A catalogue record for this book is available
from the British Library.

Typesetting and Origination by Amberley Publishing
Printed in the UK.

CONTENTS

INTRODUCTION

Katherine Willoughby is one of the most interesting women of the Tudor period.

> Muriel St Clare Byrne, *The Lisle Letters* (Chicago, 1981),
>
> vol. iv, p. 131

Katherine Suffolk was one of the most remarkable women of her time.

> Leanda de Lisle, *The Sisters Who Would Be Queen* (2010), p. 19

Katherine Willoughby is today less well known than some other Tudor ladies, but was at the forefront of the profound political and religious changes that transformed England in the reigns of King Henry VIII and his children, Edward VI, Mary I and Elizabeth I. She was born at Parham Old Hall, near Framlingham (Suffolk), in 1519, the only surviving child of William, eleventh Baron Willoughby and his wife, Maria de Salinas, a Spanish lady-in-waiting to Queen Catherine of Aragon. She inherited the family properties on her father's death in 1526, but her uncle Sir Christopher Willoughby claimed that some manors had been promised to him under the terms of an earlier settlement. The resulting dispute soured their relationship for four decades, and became the first of the many threats she would encounter in the course of her long life.

Katherine was married to Charles Brandon, Duke of Suffolk, King Henry's closest friend, at the age of just fourteen. The death of his previous wife, Henry's sister Mary, had robbed Brandon of a significant part of his income; but he loyally supported the king against the rising known as the Pilgrimage of Grace and was rewarded with authority in Lincolnshire and additional wealth in the form of lands forfeited by dissolved monasteries. Katherine became a great lady, ruling over her houses at Grimsthorpe and Tattershall, and was frequently a guest at Henry's banquets and weddings. She grew to know the king well – in 1538, only three months after Queen Jane Seymour's death, it was reported that they had been 'masking and visiting' together – and in 1543 she became a lady-in-waiting to his sixth wife Catherine Parr. Henry had a reputation for tiring of his wives once the excitement of the pursuit was over – particularly if they had failed to give him male children – and in February 1546, only six months after Charles Brandon's death, it was rumoured that the king meant to wed her himself if – and when – he could end his present marriage. Catherine Parr's Protestant religious views, which often ran contrary to the king's, were potentially treasonable, and that summer it appeared that she was about to be arrested and executed. But Henry forgave her or changed his mind at the last moment, and Katherine Willoughby never became his seventh queen. Instead she took her gentleman usher, Richard Bertie, as her second husband, and retained a degree of independence she would not have enjoyed if she had married another peer.

Katherine was by this time the most fervent of English Protestants – although her mother had been a committed Roman Catholic

– and the tragedy of losing both her sons by the duke to the 'sweating sickness' in 1551 did nothing to diminish her belief in the divine goodness. She avoided involvement in the conspiracy built around her step-granddaughter Lady Jane Grey in 1553, but was still obliged to spend four eventful years in exile in Europe beyond the reach of the Catholic Queen Mary. Here she lived from hand to mouth, gave birth to another son, and moved from city to city to avoid the attentions of the queen's agents before finally finding sanctuary in Poland. She returned home when Elizabeth succeeded, but was bitterly disappointed that the new queen's approach to religious matters was always more pragmatic and less enthusiastic than her own. Her sufferings for the Protestant cause earned her a place in Foxe's *Book of Martyrs*; her last years were clouded by her son's waywardness and her dislike of, and differences with, her daughter-in-law; and at the end she feared that Elizabeth was about to have her executed – a fear expressed in dramatic terms in her letter to the Earl of Leicester discussed in the Prologue. Hers was a life of privilege mixed with tragedy and danger, but she kept her head on her shoulders when many of her contemporaries lost theirs for less cause.

It is more than half a century since a full-length biography of Katherine was published, and the approach of the quincentenary of her birth seemed an appropriate moment to re-examine her place in Tudor history. Both previous memoirs of her have been long out of print: Lady Cecilie Goff's pioneering if rather disconnected study was published in 1930, and Evelyn Read's highly romanticised 'life' appeared in 1962. Both are based on a commendable amount of original research, but Lady Goff's book is arguably overlong – for example, she devotes many pages to events such as the Pilgrimage of Grace in which Katherine was not involved directly – while in Mrs Read's biography she seems to spend much of her time admiring the view and smelling the flowers. Both books are erratically referenced, and Mrs Read's has a very limited index.

Many accounts of individuals who lived in this period are handicapped by a lack of real evidence, but in Katherine's case the information that has survived is both personal and comparatively plentiful. Foxe's account of her sufferings for the Protestant cause and the adulatory opinions of her expressed by some of her co-religionists all need to be used with caution; but there is much of interest in the Ancaster family papers preserved in the Lincolnshire Archives and in the extant twenty-two letters she wrote to William Cecil in Edward VI's reign, followed by the same number in Queen Elizabeth's. The Ancaster documents are more formal – inventories, household accounts and the like – but her letters to Cecil give us an insight into the real Katherine – outspoken and opinionated, often complaining, sometimes having to apologise for her intemperate words or for being slow to answer, and characterised by the single-minded conviction that her view of religion was the only one acceptable to God. I have quoted freely from these documents in the belief that they give us more of the flavour of the period than would a paraphrase in my own words.

Katherine is an altogether fascinating lady. She was the wife of one Duke of Suffolk, became the mother of two others and the (step)mother-in-law of a fourth. And if the rumour that the King of Poland became enamoured of her is accurate she might have married not one monarch but two. Henry VIII, who received the title 'Defender of the Faith' from Pope Leo X when she was aged two, had broken with Rome by the time she was fifteen; and although the idea of a queen regnant was unthinkable when she was born in 1519, few would have challenged a woman's right to rule when she died in 1580. Her story is that of much of the Tudor age.

I have incurred a number of debts in the course of preparing this book, and would like to thank members of staff at the National Archives, the British Library, Lincolnshire Archives, Patrick Barker at Westhorpe and Ray Biggs at Grimsthorpe for their assistance. I am especially grateful to Nicola Tallis for reading and commenting on my manuscript, to Geoffrey Wheeler for supplying some of the illustrations and drawing the map, and to my wife Joyce for happily spending holidays visiting places associated with Katherine and for helping in many other ways.

David Baldwin

October 2014

Note: Contemporaries would have spelt the name 'Katherine' with a 'K' as opposed to a 'C'. I have referred to Katherine Willoughby as 'Katherine' throughout, but have used the alternative form for others, Catherine of Aragon, Catherine Howard, Catherine Parr, etc., to help distinguish them when their names occur together. Similarly I have consistently used the surname Willoughby, although Katherine was more properly Katherine Brandon and Katherine Bertie at different times in her life. The spelling of all quotations from contemporary letters and other documents has been modernised.

GENEALOGICAL TABLES

The **Willoughby** Family

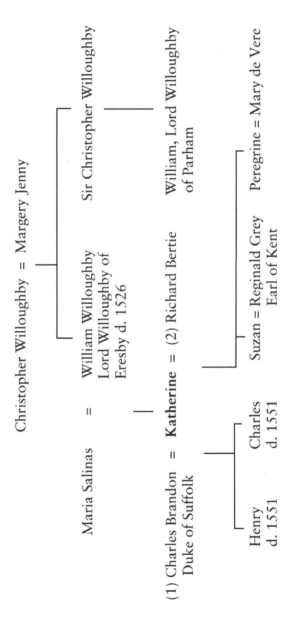

Christopher Willoughby = Margery Jenny

Maria Salinas = William Willoughby   Sir Christopher Willoughby
                  Lord Willoughby of
                  Eresby d. 1526

(1) Charles Brandon = **Katherine** = (2) Richard Bertie   William, Lord Willoughby
    Duke of Suffolk   of Parham

Henry   Charles   Suzan = Reginald Grey   Peregrine = Mary de Vere
d. 1551   d. 1551   Earl of Kent

The Descent of the Willoughby and Welles Families (Simplified)

William, 5th (V) Lord Willoughby, d. 1409

Thomas ──── Robert

Robert (VI)

Joan (VII) = Richard (VIII) ex. 1470

Lionel, Lord Welles

Cecily

Robert (IX) ex. 1470

Joan = Richard Hastings d. 1503

Christopher (X) d. 1498–9

= William (XI)

Katherine

Prologue

A MOST REMARKABLE LETTER

On a spring day in March 1580, Katherine Bertie, *née* Willoughby, dowager Duchess of Suffolk, sat down to write to Robert Dudley, Earl of Leicester, Queen Elizabeth's favourite and a powerful influence at court. Her relations with her daughter-in-law Mary, her son Peregrine's wife, had never been easy, and now Mary was spreading rumours about her which threatened more than her reputation. According to Katherine's letter, Mary had claimed that her mother-in-law was secretly trying to harm her (precisely how is not stated), and she had retaliated by circulating an earlier letter written by Katherine which appeared to call her loyalty to Elizabeth into question. Katherine was in no doubt that what she had written, presumably in all honesty, was being deliberately misinterpreted, and her letter to Dudley refers again and again to the possibility that it would result in her execution. She was by now nearly sixty, elderly by the standards of her era, and while she had not always seen eye to eye with the queen, she had never directly confronted her or thought to deprive her of her throne:

To the right honourable, & my very good lord, the earl of Leicester. I am very sorry that it is my evil fortune to be troublesome to any of my friends, specially being brought to the same by the evil hap of my dear son's marriage, by whom I had hoped to have comfort in my old days, which, by any his deserts towards me, I have found no other cause of grief than by his unadvised & unlucky choice of a fair lady [foreign] to full manners. Now, I hear by some of my friends [that she] hath in these few days, shown such a letter of mine, as doth show how near I went to lose my head, if she had not by good hap, escaped some dangers, as it seemeth, wrought to her by me. What they were, I know not. But it shall please Her Majesty to be so much my gracious lady, to appoint any to examine me of any doings towards her. I trust they shall find no likelihood in me of losing my head, nay, nor wrong in writing of my sharp letter, all circumstances considered. And as for Treason, I am sure that it is far from my heart as it could never be written by my hand. So far, I am sure, there is no cause to part my head from my body, & for felony, or murder any ways meant by me to my fair lady, as that might be a hanging matter, so I will not wish that to either of us that deserved it best, but [will] leave the revenge to God to whom I pray to deliver my innocence from wicked & most malicious slanders. I thank God, I am not the beginner of complaints, & even so I trust, by his help, in the end, if I may be heard, [that] the shame will rest where it should. But I lament that I have deserved no better of such good lady, as hath given so sad [serious] judgment of me as the loss of my head. God be praised, that hath not ordained such to take away life at the hearing of the first tale. Surely such hasty judges may be thought rather to consent to murder, than ever I shall be proved, by word, or deed, and lest I might be wrong taken in these words, I will open myself. Now, by their judgements, I escaped well that I had not lost my head. As, if I had deserved it, than it had been but just. But to give such a sentence before they proved of my deserts, must needs proceed from a murderous mind. But He that rules all & knows all, I trust will move Her Majesty's heart to think no worse of me for any such words, than she hath found me, & so, by God's grace, shall find me to the end. And this concludes with my hearty thanks to them that helped me. And being so [desirous] to you, my good Lord, to give me your good word & furtherance that I may be brought by some good means to my trial of these foul slanders (wherein I shall have cause to think myself most bounden to you), which I will pray God to requite though I cannot. And so [I] commit you to Him, from my little unwholesome house of Hampstead, whither I fled to seek quiet from these brawls, but seeing it pleaseth God to [expose] me to them even here, I now have no other shift to fly but to His special grace to give me patience to bear all these things & to keep me from deserving of shame.[1]

Katherine's prose may be convoluted, but there is no doubting her anxiety. Earlier in the letter she speaks as though she had been tried and condemned already, although her closing appeal to Dudley makes it clear that this was not the case. Her usual confidant, when she needed advice or found herself in difficulty, was William Cecil, her near-neighbour in Lincolnshire and now Elizabeth's first minister; but we may suppose that on this occasion she judged that even Cecil's influence with the queen was unlikely to prove sufficient. It would be interesting to know how Dudley responded, but regrettably his answer has not survived.

Katherine does not say precisely how she had criticised or appeared to challenge Elizabeth, but there can be little doubt that it concerned the vexed question of religion. She had written to

Cecil as early as March 1559 urging both him and the queen to embrace full-blown Protestantism, and was disappointed when they sought a settlement the majority of subjects could accept rather than one that compelled them to follow what (in Katherine's opinion) was the only right course of action. Similar, increasingly strident, missives almost certainly followed, and it is likely that it was one of these that Lady Mary brought to Elizabeth's attention. Mary's brother, the Earl of Oxford, was unhappily married to Cecil's daughter, and it is easy to see how such a letter could have found its way into the 'wrong' hands.

Today, when many people adopt a 'take it or leave it' attitude towards religion, it is not always easy to grasp how much it mattered to our sixteenth-century forebears. Acceptance of the teachings of the Church was as essential as obedience to the state, and when Henry VIII made himself head of the Church in England, religious nonconformity became potentially treasonable. Henry adopted a religion that retained some of the beliefs and practices of the old Catholic faith while rejecting others, and many of his subjects met early deaths because they could not share his view of what was, or was not, acceptable. Protestants were burned at the stake as heretics and Roman Catholics were hanged, drawn and quartered as traitors in the topsy-turvy world of Tudor England. Katherine's criticisms were concerned mainly with the pace, and extent, of the 'reform' of religion, but that, in itself, was no excuse.

It would be easy to suppose that Katherine was exaggerating, that there was really no question of her being beheaded for what amounted to a difference of opinion, but she could not assume that her age, sex and status would somehow protect her. Margaret Pole, Countess of Salisbury, Edward IV and Richard III's niece, was in her late sixties, a peeress in her own right, and a former governess to Henry VIII's daughter Princess Mary: but she had passed her royal Yorkist blood to her sons, and the increasingly paranoiac king had her executed in 1541. Margaret had been careful to avoid involvement in anything that might be construed as treasonable, and was almost certainly 'framed' by her enemies. A Parliamentary Act of Attainder obviated the need for a trial (her accusers did not have to risk having the evidence against her tested in court), and her condemnation was a foregone conclusion. Margaret's fate was one of the more extreme examples of Tudor butchery, but Katherine was right to be concerned.

Yet, in the end, there was no execution and, it would seem, no formal indictment either. Katherine's death only six months later may have precluded this, but it is perhaps more likely that Robert Dudley and William Cecil smoothed matters over. Unlike many of her religious persuasion, she died in her bed; but this daughter of a Spanish Roman Catholic mother who became the staunchest of Protestants and was included in Foxe's *Book of Martyrs* was more than just a survivor. She might even have married a king.

I

CHILDHOOD
1519–1533

Katherine Willoughby was born on 22 March 1519 at Parham Old
Hall in eastern Suffolk, the only daughter – and ultimately the only
surviving child – of William, eleventh Baron Willoughby and his
Spanish wife, Maria de Salinas. The couple had two sons, Henry,
who was possibly older than Katherine, and Francis, who may
have been named for the King of France shortly after his father
accompanied Henry VIII to the Field of the Cloth of Gold in 1520;
but both seem to have died in infancy. Like most noblemen, Lord
Willoughby would have preferred a male successor and had named
his brother Christopher his heir after his first marriage had proved
childless; but it was Katherine who succeeded to the barony when
he died in 1526.

The Willoughbys were an old peerage family with a long
tradition of service – and occasionally opposition – to the Crown.
Their ancestor Ralph had forfeited his lands for his part in the
baronial rebellion against King John, but William, the fifth
Baron Willoughby, became a trusted royal servant after helping
Henry Bolingbroke depose Richard II in 1399 (see Table 2). His

eldest son Robert, the sixth baron, fought at Agincourt and had a distinguished career as a soldier and administrator; but when he died in 1452 he left an only daughter, Joan. Joan's marriage to Richard, son and heir of Lionel, Lord Welles, temporarily united the baronies of Welles and Willoughby, and their daughter, another Joan, brought the titles to her husband Richard, younger brother of William, Lord Hastings. Richard Hastings's position was ambiguous after the House of York was defeated in 1485, and although he continued to style himself Lord Willoughby his claim was contested by his wife's kinsman Sir Christopher, the descendant of a younger son of the fifth baron. Sir Christopher predeceased Richard Hastings, but his son William, Katherine's father, became the undisputed Lord Willoughby in 1503.[1]

The period from 1455 to 1485 was the era of the Wars of the Roses, and the Willoughby and Welles families frequently found themselves on the wrong side of the argument. Lionel, Lord Welles, was slain at Towton in 1461, and ten years later his son Richard, Lord Welles and Willoughby, was executed, together with *his* son Sir Robert, for their part in the Lincolnshire rebellion against Edward IV. After the death of Robert, sixth Lord Willoughby, in 1452 his widow, Maud Stanhope, married Sir Thomas Neville who was killed with the Duke of York at Wakefield, and then wed, as her third husband, Sir Gervase Clifton, who was executed after the Battle of Tewkesbury in 1471. By this time she had apparently had enough of matrimony, and stayed single for the remaining twenty-six years of her life.

The wars were over when Katherine's father succeeded to the barony at the turn of the century, and he became one of Henry VII's most committed supporters. Invited to formally welcome Catherine of Aragon to England in November 1501, he later escorted Princess Margaret to York when she wed James IV of Scotland, and was appointed Master of the Hart Hounds in July 1508. He was frequently employed in campaigns against the French in the young Henry VIII's reign, and part of his reward was to make two conspicuously good marriages. His first wife, Mary, sister of John Lord Hussey, died young, and he wed Maria (Mary) de Salinas, one of Queen Catherine's Spanish ladies-in-waiting, in June 1516. The king attended the wedding (where he offered 6s 8d), granted the couple the reversion of Grimsthorpe and other Lincolnshire manors forfeited to the Crown by Francis Lovel, Richard III's friend and chamberlain, and named one of his new ships the *Mary Willoughby*.

Maria was one of only two fellow Spaniards whose services the queen retained on her marriage to King Henry, and the Spanish ambassador complained bitterly that she was encouraging her mistress to put England's interests before those of her father King Ferdinand. 'The few Spaniards who are still in her household,' he wrote, 'prefer to be friends of the English, and neglect their duties as subjects of the King of Spain. The worst influence on the queen is exercised by Dona Maria de Salinas, whom she loves more than any other mortal.'² He may have exaggerated, but Catherine and Maria were undoubtedly close.

Henry VIII had become king on his father's death in 1509, but might never have done so if his elder brother Arthur, Catherine of Aragon's first husband, had not died unexpectedly in 1502. Good-looking and athletic, he wed Catherine himself shortly after his accession, and for many years they seemed ideally suited. He was deservedly popular, but his ruthlessness, his readiness to send Yorkists and other descendants of Edward III to the block, soon manifested itself. Edmund de la Pole, Earl of Suffolk, executed in 1513, and Edward Stafford, Duke of Buckingham, beheaded in 1521, were only the first of a long line of rival claimants who were destined to be eliminated during the years he ruled England. Parliament had acquired certain powers – most notably the right to vote taxation – but the king was still his own prime minister and pursued his own foreign policy. He was the fount of all political authority, and in the next decade would assume control over religious matters too.

Katherine grew up in a country that, in many ways, still resembled the England of the Middle Ages, but was experiencing some profound if subtle changes. Printed books, which had first become available at the end of the fifteenth century, were being produced in ever larger quantities and made knowledge accessible to everyone who could read. Already there were demands for an English Bible, and soon anyone with a little education would be able to challenge the teachings of the Church. The great Gothic period of church building succumbed to the Reformation after 1530, and nobles and gentlemen who no longer needed the protection of castles and moated houses began to make their homes more impressive and comfortable. The common living space of the great hall was partitioned, and high, draughty ceilings were lowered to create new private rooms at first-floor level. Wood panelling and hanging tapestries countered the cold of stone or brickwork, but glass remained expensive and large sheets could be manufactured only with difficulty. It is likely that small windows made many of the rooms Katherine occupied dim and airless, and that she seldom missed an opportunity to exchange the confines of the house for the garden. Once, all land attached to a dwelling would have been used for growing herbs and fruit and for other utilitarian purposes, but the rich were now creating pleasure gardens featuring geometric flowerbeds and low hedges. It was all part of what they believed was a more cultivated, and more 'civilised', way of life.

Katherine would have readily appreciated these innovations, but other changes affecting society would only become apparent later. The Black Death and other disasters had reduced the population of England and Wales from somewhere between four and five million to about two million by the middle of the fifteenth century and recovery was slow. England alone still had only an estimated two and a quarter million inhabitants by 1525, but growth accelerated rapidly thereafter, reaching perhaps two and three-quarter million by 1541. The increased demand benefited those able to meet it, but for others the inevitable speculation in land and foodstuffs led to inflation, unemployment, poverty, vagrancy and urban squalor. If a basket of consumables cost 100 in the period 1451–75, it had risen to 111 in 1519–20 (the year of Katherine's birth), and to a staggering 148 by the end of the next decade. Modern governments often have little success in tackling this problem, and their Tudor counterparts fared no better. Henry VIII would not have thought that trying to control economic – or demographic and social – changes formed any part of his responsibilities towards his subjects. They were simply 'acts of God'.[3]

Lord and Lady Willoughby's obligations to the king and queen meant that they were only periodically at home as a family, and they would always have seemed more distant to little Katherine than the nurses and teachers who were responsible for her well-being and whom she saw every day. No precise evidence for this, the earliest phase of her life, has come down to us, but her education and upbringing would have mirrored the routines of other girls whose parents moved in the same social circles. Her day would have begun with mass or formal prayers at dawn followed by breakfast – consisting of bread, eggs and sometimes mutton washed down with small beer or ale. She would then have gone to her studies, reading and writing, perhaps memorising Latin passages from the Bible, and acquiring the ability to converse with other members of polite society in French, until dinner, the main meal of the day, was served between eleven and one. After dinner there would be more pleasant lessons, learning to ride a horse, to dance, to sew, to play a musical instrument and, most importantly, good manners. Supper would have been at about five or six according to the season, and would have been followed by games and recreation before more prayers and bed. Discipline could be harsh – Katherine would later order 'byrche for roddes' to chastise her own children[4] – and privacy was almost non-existent. She would have become sexually aware long before the more sheltered children of some later eras.

Katherine's father died in October 1526, some six months after his daughter's seventh birthday. The cause of death is unknown, but if the assumption by *The Complete Peerage* that he was 'probably of age' (i.e. twenty-one) by November 1497 is accurate he would have been at least fifty, a good lifespan for that period. Her mourning was perhaps more formal than personal, but the fact that she was now an heiress and a ward of the Crown was bound to affect her future. Lord Willoughby's closest surviving male relative was his brother Sir Christopher Willoughby, and Sir Christopher now claimed that the promises made to him before Katherine's birth entitled him to some of the family properties.[5] The result was an acrimonious dispute in which Sir Christopher asserted his right to the lands in the courts of Chancery and Star Chamber while simultaneously occupying Eresby and threatening to seize other manors. Lady Willoughby petitioned Queen Catherine and took the precaution of removing certain valuables from Parham; but an agreement of sorts was reached only after Charles Brandon, Duke of Suffolk, bought Katherine's wardship from King Henry (for £2,266 13s 4d) in March 1528. Brandon acted to protect what were now his – as well as Katherine's – interests, and although Sir Christopher was allowed to keep certain properties he was denied others. He believed that his niece and her allies had cheated him, and ill feeling lingered for many years.

Charles Brandon was the son of Sir William Brandon, the knight killed bearing Henry VII's standard at the Battle of Bosworth, and owed his rapid rise in the world entirely to his friendship – and camaraderie – with Henry VIII. Steven Gunn has remarked that in 1509 Charles was one of ninety-three esquires of the body in the funeral procession of Henry VII; but five years later he was Charles, Duke of Suffolk, by Tudor rules of precedence Henry VIII's fifth most exalted subject.[6] His skill as a jouster and his ability to share the king's pleasures ensured that he remained close to Henry, and – unlike many senior royal servants – he died in his bed.

Brandon's marital liaisons were almost as numerous as those of his royal master, and no less complicated. In 1503 or slightly later, he promised to marry Anne Browne, a daughter of the Constable of Calais, Sir Anthony Browne, and by her had a daughter named Anne. The marriage did not proceed, however, and he sought to improve his prospects by wedding Lady Margaret Neville, a daughter of John, Marquis Montagu, Warwick the Kingmaker's brother, who was many years his senior. He had licence to enter Margaret's lands in February 1507, and from a series of sales raised over £1,000 (which he doubtless pocketed) before seeking annulment of the union on the grounds that they were too closely related to have been legally married in the first place.[7] He wed Anne Browne in 1508 and they had a second daughter, Mary, two years later; but her death shortly afterwards presented him with new opportunities. He bought the wardship of the young Lady Lisle and was allowed to assume her title on the understanding that he intended to marry her; but this did not prevent him from flirting with Margaret of Austria, the regent of the Netherlands, when King Henry visited her court in 1513. There can be no doubt that he was keeping his options open, and any possibility that he would espouse either of these ladies evaporated when he married Mary, the king's younger sister, in February 1515.

It is unclear when Brandon first formed an attachment to Mary, but it was certainly before she was married to Louis XII, the elderly King of France, in the summer of 1514. Louis expired the following January, and Mary and Brandon wed in Paris in mid-February without first obtaining her brother's permission. Henry may not have been particularly surprised – he is said to have assured Mary that, if Louis died, she could marry someone of her own choosing, and he knew that Brandon was enamoured of her – but the implication was that his sister feared he would renege on his promise if another Continental alliance beckoned. Brandon excused himself by claiming that he 'newar sawe woman soo wyepe' (when she begged him to marry her),[8] and Mary made their peace with Henry by agreeing to give him her jewels and plate, half her dowry and a further £24,000 drawn from her dower lands in France payable over twelve years. The price of rehabilitation was massive, but Brandon was surely mindful of the fact that a child of his might one day succeed the still childless king.

Brandon and Mary returned to England to marry again at

Greenwich – this time with royal approval – and to establish themselves as a great lord and lady in East Anglia. They engaged in extensive rebuilding projects – notably at Suffolk Place, their town house in Southwark, and at Westhorpe in Suffolk – and were again leaders of society when the nine-year-old Katherine Willoughby joined their household in 1528. By now they had two daughters of their own, Frances, who was almost two years older than Katherine, and Eleanor, about the same age, as well as a son, Henry, born in 1522 and created Earl of Lincoln in 1525. Sixteenth-century parents regularly sent their children to the homes of others to complete their education (while taking the children of their social equals into their own houses), and a practice that may appear uncaring to our way of thinking would have seemed perfectly normal at that period. The aim was to teach a girl like Katherine how to run a great household herself, how to behave in polite society, and, perhaps most importantly, give her an opportunity to forge relationships that would stand her in good stead when she grew older. She soon formed an attachment to Frances, and her friends in the Westhorpe household included Margaret Douglas, the daughter of King Henry's elder sister Margaret and her second husband the Earl of Angus.

Katherine disappears from the record for the next few years – her daily routine would have seemed hardly worth mentioning – but great events were unfolding in the world beyond Suffolk. Queen Catherine had given her husband a number of children, but only one, Princess Mary, born in 1516, had survived infancy. By the mid-1520s her childbearing years were clearly behind her, and Henry, who desperately wanted a son to succeed him, came to regard an annulment of the marriage as not merely desirable but necessary. He chose to believe that he had offended God by marrying his late brother Arthur's widow (the Old Testament book of Leviticus specifically forbade such a union), and that childlessness – the prescribed penalty – had been visited upon him even though he had a daughter. His problem was that the book of Deuteronomy appeared to state the opposite – that a man *should* marry his brother's widow and 'raise up seed unto his brother' – a problem the royal theologians overcame by arguing that the word 'brother' in Deuteronomy meant all male relatives except for brothers-in-law who were specifically excluded by Leviticus. Henry, they reasoned, was not childless in the accepted sense of the word, but critically, had no son to carry on his name.[9]

It is not easy to decide at what point Henry's infatuation with Anne Boleyn became a factor in his calculations, but there can be no doubt that her refusal to become his mistress made him more determined than ever to remarry. The Pope was too afraid of the Emperor Charles V (who was Catherine of Aragon's nephew) to grant Henry the annulment he wanted, and finally, between 1530 and 1533, Henry made his own solution on his own terms. The new 'Supreme Head of the Church in England' had his marriage to Queen Catherine declared unlawful in May 1533, and Anne was crowned in her place on 1 June.

The changes imposed by King Henry were bound to affect the lives of many members of the aristocracy, and Katherine Willoughby's new family had good reason to regret some of them. Charles Brandon was delegated to inform Catherine that she was no longer queen, and in December 1533 was instructed to dismiss some of her servants and move her from Buckden in Huntingdonshire to Somersham in the Isle of Ely against her will. He found these tasks distasteful – if Eustace Chapuys, the Imperial ambassador, is to be believed, he 'wished some mischief might happen to him to excuse himself from this journey' – but could not defy the king who had raised him from nothing.[10] Mary, his wife, had a poor opinion of Mistress Boleyn, and had declined to accompany the royal couple to Calais to meet King Francis in 1532. It was a most unhappy period, and Katherine must have felt that a cloud had descended on her guardian's house.

By 1533 Katherine was approaching her fourteenth birthday, and her horizons were broadened when she saw and met many of the great and good of the kingdom (possibly for the first time) at Anne Boleyn's coronation. Mary Brandon had been unwell for some time and returned to Westhorpe almost immediately afterwards, but her husband remained in London, perhaps to facilitate arrangements for the marriage of Frances, their elder daughter, to Henry Grey, Marquis of Dorset.[11] Katherine may have accompanied Mary or stayed with Brandon; but if the latter then her sojourn in the capital ended abruptly when the duke received word that Mary's health was failing. They made their excuses and rode hard for East Anglia, but failed to reach her before she died on 25 June. Her dislike of Queen Anne had been shared by Maria Willoughby and, in all probability, by Katherine herself.

Mary's funeral was conducted with all the respect due to a lady who was both a dowager Queen of France and a senior member of the English royal family. Her body, embalmed and placed in a leaden coffin covered by a pall of blue velvet, lay in state in the chapel at Westhorpe for more than three weeks while arrangements were made for her burial. Her former attendants watched over her, tapers burned constantly and Mass was said every day. According to custom, the deceased's closest female relative, her eldest daughter Frances, acted as chief mourner, and on Tuesday

21 July she was formally escorted to the chapel by her brother, the Earl of Lincoln, and her husband, the Marquis of Dorset. Also in attendance, and walking behind in couples, were Eleanor Brandon and Katherine, followed by Anne, Lady Powis, and Mary, Lady Monteagle, Charles Brandon's daughters by Anne Browne. Mass was said, and after the bereaved had made their offerings they breakfasted while the cortège was prepared for its journey to Bury. Six gentlemen conveyed the coffin from its resting place in the chapel to the funeral car which was richly draped with black velvet embroidered with escutcheons of Mary's arms and drawn by six horses. A pall of cloth of gold of frieze (a heavy woollen fabric) on a black ground was thrown over the coffin, with a cross of the same on a white ground incorporating a portrait showing her apparelled in her state robes, wearing a crown of gold upon her head and holding a sceptre in her right hand.

When everything was in order, the procession began. At its head walked a hundred poor men in black gowns and hoods, each carrying a wax taper, followed by the clergy of the chapel with the cross. Next came barons, knights and gentlemen, the officers of the deceased's household, Garter and Clarenceux kings of arms, and Lord Powis, Mary's chamberlain, all on horses draped with black cloth. The funeral car, surrounded by a hundred yeomen with torches, preceded the Lady Frances who was mounted on a horse covered with trappings of black velvet, the Marquis of Dorset riding on her right hand and Lord Clifford (Eleanor's husband) on her left. Behind them, in single file, rode ten noble ladies on horseback, each bareheaded and attended by a lackey; then came two mourning chariots, the female attendants of the deceased on foot, and lastly, a number of yeomen and servants with 'all other that would', i.e. all who wished to follow as unbidden guests.

At two o'clock in the afternoon the cortège reached Bury and was met by the priests of the parish, 'in their best ornaments, doing such ceremonies as to the same appertaineth'. Proceeding to the abbey, it was received at the first gate by the abbot and monks and at the second by the Bishop of London and other prelates wearing their pontifical robes. The coffin was transferred from the car to a hearse hung with black sarcenet (fine silk) with fringes of silk and gold, and bearing the deceased's arms and device in fine gold with her motto *La volonté de Dieu me suffit* (The will of God is sufficient for me). Draperies of black cloth, garnished with escutcheons, lined the passage and the pillars of the church all the way to the high altar, a mark of respect that would have provided the suppliers and workshops of the town with much employment. When the mourners were arranged in their respective places, the dirge was solemnly chanted by the clergy, and 'at the times accustomed' a pursuivant sent from France to assist the English heralds cried, 'Pray for the soul of the right high excellent princess and right Christian Queen, Mary, late French queen, and all Christian souls.'

At the conclusion of the ceremony the invited guests adjourned to the great chamber of the monastery where a plentiful supper was provided 'in goodly order and sort as could be devised with all manner of delicacies'. A chosen company of mourners watched round the hearse that night, and two Masses were said early the next morning. After breakfast the whole party walked to the chapel in order of precedence to attend requiem Mass and present their offerings. The ladies Powis and Monteagle, the two ladies Willoughby (Katherine and her mother), and the ladies Eleanor and Frances Brandon received splendid palls of cloth of gold from the hands of the kings of arms, and carried them to the foot of the coffin where the Garter king placed them in position. The ladies returned to their places, the abbot of St Benet's preached the sermon, and the service came to an end.

The coffin was carried to the place of burial, beneath a gorgeous canopy with banners waving, and slowly lowered; whereupon the senior members of the deceased's household broke in two their staves of office and 'with great weeping and lamentation' cast them into the grave. The solemnities of the interment being ended, all departed to dinner, and 'after dinner everybody took their leave that would, and had great thanks full gently'. 'There was also provided for the poor people a great dole in four places in the town of Bury, having meats and drinks, come who would, and every poor body [received] 4*d*'.¹²

The funeral of a woman she had no doubt come to admire must have been a sad day for Katherine, but it would have made her realise that she was now old enough to be an active participant in a great ceremony and that her childhood days were behind her. So far, she would have had few opportunities to meet or observe King Henry. Ladies-in-waiting did not take their children to court with them,¹³ and her first glimpse of him may have been when he visited the Suffolks at Ewelme in Oxfordshire in July 1532. She would have seen him again if, as seems likely, he attended Frances and Henry Grey's wedding (and her own for that matter), but protocol obliged him to remain aloof from Queen Anne's coronation and his sister's funeral. What Katherine thought of him on the rare occasions she did encounter him is not recorded, but she would have seen a man already in his early forties with a figure very different to that of the handsome youth who had ascended the throne twenty-four years earlier. Sumptuously dressed, he was magnificent after a manner of speaking and perhaps rather frightening, a man who could do – and have – what he wanted. She could never have imagined that one day he might want her.

2

THE BRANDON MARRIAGE
1533–1545

One of the rights Charles Brandon acquired when he bought Katherine's wardship was to marry her to a man of his own choosing. It was assumed that he intended her as a bride for his son, the eleven-year-old Henry, Earl of Lincoln, but in September 1533, only ten weeks after Mary's death, he wed her himself. This was an era in which early remarriage, and marriage between youth and age, were commonplace, and the speed with which the wedding was arranged is no more likely to have raised eyebrows than the fact that a forty-nine-year-old man was marrying a fourteen-year-old girl. Catherine Parr was joined to Lord Thomas Seymour a mere four months after Henry VIII died in 1547, and when Chapuys wrote to inform Charles V that the Duke of Suffolk was to marry Lady Willoughby's daughter 'next Sunday', he jocularly remarked that 'in contracting such a marriage, the duke will no doubt please the ladies of this country, who, imitating his example, will no doubt take their revenge, when accused of marrying again immediately after the death of their husbands, as they are in the habit of doing'.[1]

We do not know how Katherine received Brandon's proposal, but she had been brought up to believe that making a 'good' marriage was more important than mutual affection. In his youth the duke had been a fine athlete and had cut an impressive figure; but now he was becoming stout and would be described a very few years later as 'a good man and captain, but sickly and half lame'.[2] He was old enough to be Katherine's grandfather, but the passing of the years had not affected his ability to flatter or make playful advances to a pretty girl. As early as 1531 rumours emanating from Anne Boleyn's household suggested that the duke's interest in his young ward was more than paternal, and although allowance must be made for Anne's poor relationship with the Brandons there is seldom smoke without fire. Brandon, for his part, surely relished the opportunity to espouse this nubile, attractive teenager, but the attraction was more than sexual. The Earl of Lincoln was ailing – he died six months later in 1534 – and even if he had wed Katherine her estates would have been lost to the Brandon family when she remarried. Instead, they remained firmly in Charles Brandon's keeping, and Katherine's youth could only improve his chances of fathering another son to inherit them. Later commentators hinted that young Lincoln died of grief when his father 'stole' his intended, but they were probably being wise after the event.

According to Chapuys, Katherine and Charles Brandon were married on 7 September, almost certainly in London and very probably in the presence of the king.[3] We can be reasonably certain of this because only three days later Brandon 'supported' the old Duchess of Norfolk when she stood godmother to the infant Princess Elizabeth. Elizabeth's baptism would have been Katherine's first formal appearance as Duchess of Suffolk, and marks the beginning of what was to be a long and not always easy relationship with the future sovereign. But no one, least of all Katherine, would have guessed this on a late summer's day in 1533.

No detailed account of the wedding has come down to us but we may assume that, in accordance with tradition, the couple exchanged vows and the groom placed a ring on the fourth finger of the bride's left hand 'in plain sight' at the church door. They then entered the building where their marriage was blessed and wine – a symbol of the new bond between the two families – was served to the assembled guests. The ceremony was followed by a feast – usually at the bride's home but perhaps on this occasion at Suffolk Place – and then by consummation. There was frequently much horseplay as the newly-wed couple were put to bed, but such revelries were part of the occasion. Katherine would not have been surprised or alarmed.

How Katherine coped with her new role and responsibilities can only be imagined, but she cannot have found it easy. Until very recently she had been the heiress to a barony and the ward of one of the most powerful men in England; now she was his wife, a duchess, and the mistress of his household. At court she could allow her husband to take the lead while she basked in his evident pride in her, but she could not expect him to shield her when they were 'at home' in London or at Westhorpe. The servants would have been used to treating her with the respect due to a girl in her former position, but how did they respond to this abrupt change in their relationship? Some, no doubt, laughed behind their hands when she made mistakes (as she was almost bound to do in the early days), but they knew their places and Katherine would have learned fast.

Her relationship with her husband can scarcely have been one of equals, but she fulfilled her principal duty admirably when she presented him with a healthy son two years after their marriage on 18 September 1535. King Henry stood godfather at the infant's baptism and gave him his own name, but Katherine would not have been present. Contemporaries believed that a newborn child must be baptised at the earliest opportunity (or his soul would not go to heaven if he happened to die), and even if the mother had recovered sufficiently from her ordeal to attend the service she would not have been permitted to do so until she had been 'churched', cleansed of her ritual impurity, forty days after the birth. The king gave the midwife and nurse responsible for the child's well-being the generous sum of £4.

Giving birth in the early Tudor period was governed by a well-defined ritual. About four to six weeks before the expected delivery the mother-to-be would be confined to her chamber where she would be attended only by women. The room would be richly furnished, fresh air, which was thought to be harmful at such a time, would be excluded as far as possible, and holy relics believed to be efficacious in such circumstances would be borrowed in readiness. The risks involved were considerable – almost everyone would have known, or known of, a woman who had died in childbed – but were perhaps no greater than those posed by the many untreatable illnesses of the period. Katherine would have been confined to bed for three days after the birth and the room kept dark – because labour was thought to weaken the eyesight. She would then progress to 'upsitting' and to walking within, and later without, her chamber, but she would not go outside until after she had been churched.

Katherine's daily life, the food she ate, the clothes she wore, and other personal matters, would have been akin to those of other great ladies of the era. Fresh food was available only in season, and cooks regularly used herbs and more costly imported spices to improve the flavour of meat that had been salted or was already deteriorating. The number of dishes served at mealtimes was a status symbol regulated by statute – a duke like Brandon was entitled to seven courses, a cardinal nine, and an abbot six, for example. Numerous comestibles were provided – the more unusual and expensive the better – and presentation was everything. A peacock might be served stuffed but whole, with all its wonderful plumage, and confections sometimes achieved architectural proportions. It was the time-honoured concept of largesse – prodigious expenditure to make a point – and nothing could be done 'on the cheap'.

Beautiful clothes made from expensive materials also emphasised the wearer's status, and medieval 'sumptuary laws' still determined who could, or could not, wear certain items according to their place in society. Katherine's basic attire would have consisted of a chemise (the basic undergarment), wool or silk stockings, one or more petticoats, a kirtle (an ankle-length sleeveless dress with attachable sleeves of different patterns), a rich overgown (parted at the front to reveal the kirtle), and a headdress. Jewellery gave her appearance its finishing touches, and perfumes allowed her to mix easily in polite society. How often she bathed or washed herself must remain conjectural. Alison Sim argues that, contrary to popular belief, Tudor people tried to keep themselves as clean as they could in the circumstances. The real problem, she suggests, lay in close-fitting garments made from costly fabrics that could not be laundered and became offensive on hot days in summer.[4]

Keeping a large establishment sweet and disposing of waste was as problematic as personal hygiene, perhaps more so, but no one appreciated the extent to which dirt could adversely affect peoples' health. They believed that bad smells could cause illness, but had no understanding of bacterial infections or of how microbes thrived on filth. If plague or another epidemic broke out the only solution was to move away, although this in itself risked spreading the disease to another area. Katherine was fortunate that none of her pregnancies proved fatal, and that she did not suffer an injury, perhaps while out riding, that necessitated surgery. The only anaesthetics available – opium and hemlock – could kill even before the surgeon had begun to operate, and there was no remedy if gangrene set in afterwards. The two most feared illnesses were smallpox – which scarred the 50 per cent of sufferers who survived it – and the so-called sweating sickness, which is thought to have been brought to England by Henry Tudor's soldiers in 1485. It recurred at regular intervals until 1551 and would have a devastating impact on Katherine herself.

Katherine and her husband undoubtedly enjoyed the best of everything that was available, but Brandon's financial difficulties – coupled with the king's determination to pursue what were, for them, unwelcome policies – meant that there were periods when life was distinctly uncomfortable. Their main problem was that many of the forfeited estates of the former de la Pole dukes of Suffolk had been given to others or were burdened with dower interests, and Brandon received only approximately 35 per cent of them (in terms of value) in 1514 and 1515.[5] The dower interests would revert to him sooner or later and he could try to buy or lease back other properties, but in the meantime he was obliged to maintain a ducal lifestyle on a reduced landed income. The payments he received from his offices and wardships helped of course, but they could not compensate for the loss of his wife Mary's French dower, worth about £4,000 per annum under the terms of his arrangement with his royal brother-in-law. This had ceased on her death, and to make matters worse he was obliged to surrender property and exchange Suffolk Place together with the reversion of Westhorpe for less desirable houses when Henry demanded a final settlement. Katherine's lands brought in £900 a year, but her husband, who had had to borrow large sums to make ends meet even when he was married to Mary, would have had little room for manoeuver. There were inevitably occasions when they had to stall creditors and pretend that money was not as tight as it was.

Then there was Catherine of Aragon, now kept forlorn and isolated at Kimbolton in Cambridgeshire, still stoically refusing to accept that she was no longer Henry's wife and queen. By the end of 1535 she was dying, and Maria Willoughby's requests to visit her former mistress fell on deaf ears. Undaunted, Maria left London before dawn on New Year's Eve, and after falling from her horse and being told (mistakenly) that Catherine was already dead reached Kimbolton at about six o'clock the following evening. The keeper, Sir Edmund Bedingfield, had been told to admit no one to the house without authority, but she showed him the bruises she had sustained on the journey and begged him for the love of Jesus and Christian charity to allow her to come in and warm herself by the fire. Sir Edmund relented, and Maria then pleaded to be allowed to see her mistress, claiming that a letter which would show that the king had no objection would arrive shortly. Once inside the queen's rooms she was safe; and a week later, on 7 January, Catherine died in her arms.

So it was that Katherine and her mother found themselves attending the funeral of a second former queen less than three years after that of the first. The obsequies were similar to those performed for Mary, except that on this occasion Katherine was the most senior mourner after Lady Eleanor Brandon. Queen Catherine had requested burial in a chapel of the Observant Friars, but her wishes were disregarded and she was laid to rest in Peterborough Abbey. The sermon was preached by John Hilsey, bishop-designate of Rochester, who

> preached the same as all the preachers of England for two years have not ceased to preach, viz., against the power of the Pope, whom they call bishop of Rome, and against the marriage of the said good Queen [Catherine] and the King, alleging against all truth that in the hour of death she acknowledged she had not been Queen of England.[6]

Catherine had always rejected the pretence that she had never been more than a dowager Princess of Wales (Henry's brother Arthur's widow) – and the sermon would have disgusted the Willoughby ladies as much as it would undoubtedly have offended her.

Nothing could now right the wrong done to Queen Catherine, but Katherine and her mother may have felt some satisfaction when Anne Boleyn fell from grace and was beheaded less than four months later. Anne was naturally flirtatious, but historians agree that the charges brought against her – having sexual relations with five courtiers, one of them her own brother – were contrived and spurious. It has been suggested that Henry had been fascinated by her unattainability, her refusal to become his mistress, and lost interest in her once the excitement of the chase was over. But her real 'crime' was that, like Catherine before her, she had failed to give him a son.

Henry married his third wife Jane Seymour on 30 May 1536, only eleven days after Anne's execution, and there was another grand wedding just over a month later when three young noblemen, John de Vere, Lord Bulbeck, Henry Neville, son of the Earl of Westmoreland, and Henry Manners, Lord Roos, were married at Shoreditch. Brandon was certainly present on the second occasion, and it is likely that he and Katherine attended both ceremonies. The chronicler Charles Wriothesley describes how

all these three lords were married at one mass, going to church all three together, and the ladies, their wives, following one after another, every one of the young ladies having two young lords going on every side of them, and a young lady bearing up every [one] of their gown trains. At which marriage was present all the great estates of the realm, both lords and ladies; the Lord Chancellor of England and the Duke of Norfolk leading the Lord Bulbeck's wife home from the church, the Duke of Suffolk and the Lord Marquis of Dorset leading the Lord Neville's wife, and the Earl of Derby and the Earl of Surrey leading the Lord Roos's wife. And after Mass, there was a great dinner and diverse great dishes and delicate meats with subtleties [delicacies] and diverse manner of instruments playing at the same, which were too long to express [describe]. And after dinner the King's Grace came thither in a mask, riding from York Place, with eleven more with him, whereof the King and seven more with him wore garments after the Turkish fashion, richly embroidered with gold, with Turkish hats of black velvet and white feathers on their heads, and visors on their faces; and four others were arrayed in purple sarcenet, like Turks, which were as their pages. And so they danced with the ladies a good while; and then the King put off his visor and showed himself; and then the King had a great banquet of forty dishes, wherein was diverse subtleties and meats, which was a goodly sight to behold. The banquet ended, the King with his company departed thence, and rode again to York Place in their masking garments as they came thither.[7]

The king enjoyed 'disguising' himself, and the guests would have had the good sense to look surprised when his identity was 'revealed'.

Henry's break with Rome allowed Protestants in his government – men like Thomas Cromwell and Archbishop Thomas Cranmer – to seek to eradicate forms of worship, praying to saints and the veneration of relics for example, that they regarded as mere superstition. They can hardly be blamed for seizing their opportunity, but what they failed to appreciate was the extent to which most conservative Catholic Englishmen believed their beloved old religion was being dismantled. Henry's religious changes in general, and the dissolution of some monasteries in particular, were seen as 'alien and southern' innovations by many inhabitants of the more traditionally minded north and east of the country, and the ten 'New Articles of Religion' introduced in the summer of 1536 proved violently unpopular. Many of the old holidays, particularly those which fell at harvest time, were abolished, and there were loud complaints that 'they [the Articles] treated of no more than three sacraments (baptism, marriage and communion), where always the people had been taught seven' (these three plus penance, holy orders, confirmation and extreme unction).

Few would have disputed that the reform of at least the smaller monasteries was desirable, but there was bitter opposition to the wider destruction of an institution that had long helped poor people in times of trouble. Discontent in the south was less formidable but it was still present. A preacher at Sturminster Newton in Dorset told the people to keep their old holidays, to continue to light candles, and to 'beware of heretics and reading this New Testament in English' while another said that 'if the king didn't go to Hell it was because Satan didn't live there'. Anne Boleyn's alleged lovers were widely regarded as victims – 'put to death only for pleasure' in the words of one John Hill of Oxford, who also remarked that he 'hoped to see the King of Scots King of England'. On another level Henry's cousin, Cardinal Reginald Pole, sent him a book entitled *De Unitae Ecclesiae*, described as 'unpleasant, blistering and disrespectful', in which he compared the king to Emperor Nero and accused him of 'tearing like a wild beast' men like the executed Sir Thomas More 'who were the greatest honour to the kingdom'. He suggested – as a final insult – that Henry, who prided himself on his theological knowledge, should appoint an expert to read the book and give him an unbiased opinion of it. The king stifled his anger and invited Pole to England to talk things over, but the cardinal was too cautious to come.

By the autumn of 1536 Lincolnshire and the north were seething with discontent as the plundering of the smaller monasteries seemed to confirm the populace's worst fears. On Sunday 1 October, at Louth, the administrative centre of northern Lincolnshire, the local vicar Thomas Kendall preached a rousing sermon denouncing the reforms, and within days much of the county was up in arms.[8] The rebels demanded, among other things, reconciliation with Rome, the reversal of all the recent religious innovations, and the removal of the 'lowborn' councillors who they believed were responsible for them, but Henry was having none of it. 'How presumptuous ye are,' he wrote, 'the rude commons of one shire, and that the most brute and beastly of the whole realm, to find fault with your prince.' It was Parliament, not Cromwell, which had decreed the Dissolution of the Monasteries, and he could not, and would not, grant such an unreasonable petition. He instructed Charles Brandon to raise troops to quell the protests 'to destroy burn and kill man woman and child if necessary' and the rising collapsed as the duke's army approached.

The king doubtless hoped that this would be the end of the matter, but no sooner had the trouble in Lincolnshire been dealt with than a new, and potentially far more serious, threat to royal authority engulfed much of northern England. The 'Pilgrimage of Grace for the Commonweal', led by Robert Aske, a capable lawyer and local squire, repeated the petitions of the Lincolnshire rebels, and further demanded that no man living north of the Trent should be compelled to attend any court except York. Aske established himself in Pontefract Castle, and soon had an army boasting four peers, many gentry, and 30,000 ordinary people (many of them 'warlike men and well appointed') at his back. The Duke of Norfolk, Henry's commander in the region, decided not to risk a battle and instead persuaded the 'Pilgrims' that the king would forgive them and listen sympathetically to their grievances if they dispersed quietly. Norfolk rode to London taking two of the rebels with him, and they returned with the offer of a free pardon, a new Parliament to re-examine the religious changes, and an invitation to Aske to discuss the matter with Henry personally. The meeting went well, and Aske felt so sure of the king's goodwill that in January 1537 he took the bold step of ordering his followers to disband. But no sooner was the crisis over than he was made prisoner, dragged on a hurdle through York, and hung in chains.

Henry's revenge continued throughout the spring and summer. In Yorkshire abbots and local gentlemen were among those executed, while thirty-six of the commons were hanged in Lincolnshire together with seventy-four in Carlisle. 'You shall in any wise,' wrote Henry, 'cause such dreadful execution to be done upon a good number of the inhabitants of every town, village and hamlet that have been offenders in the rebellion, as well by hanging them up in trees as by quartering of them and the setting of their heads and quarters in every town, great and small, as they may be a fearful spectacle to all other hereafter that would practice a like manner.' The Pilgrims fell into the trap of believing that the king was, in a sense, one of them, that he was genuinely concerned for their well-being and happiness, and that their grievances were the fault of others. They failed to appreciate that, in reality, nothing could be done without royal approval, and that the religious changes were essentially Henry's even if Cromwell and others drove them forward. Their naivety, their rather touching faith in the goodness of the Lord's anointed, appears vaguely absurd to our way of thinking, but they could conceive of no other form of government. The blind trust (in Richard II) which had been the ruin of Wat Tyler's rebels in 1381 proved the Pilgrims' nemesis in 1536.

The Pilgrims had wanted to turn back the religious clock, but their failure only hastened the destruction of the greater monasteries and with them the whole ethos of medieval monastic life in England. The monks of these houses, who Parliament had previously accepted 'kept and observed religion right well', were accused of encouraging their tenants to join the uprising, and abbots who resisted the royal will were severely punished. Some became martyrs for the faith to which they were devoted, but the majority kept both their lives and their incomes. Those who opted to retire gracefully were granted livings or received generous pensions, and a few heads of houses may have shared the relief of the abbot of Beaulieu, who commented, 'Thank God I am rid of my lewd monks.' Katherine may have known Abbot Reeve of Bury St Edmunds, described as 'a merry old man, fond of the ladies, fond of his glass, fond of the gardens of his country houses' who was allowed the generous sum of 500 marks (£333 6s 8d) per annum, but who died of old age within six months.

Charles Brandon had been ordered to remain in Lincoln to prevent further trouble in the eastern counties unless the situation in the north became critical, and Katherine was able to keep in touch with him by letter and to join him in person later. In October 1536 she wrote to inform him that there was a 'great bruit' (rumour) in Suffolk that the king's army had been defeated and that the government meant to seize poor people's cattle (a curious contrast), and they were together by 7 December when Brandon told Henry that he intended to come to court at Christmas, 'leaving his wife in these parts'.[9] It is likely that she was again heavily pregnant since one authority has it that Charles, their second son, was born early the following year.

When King Henry created Brandon Duke of Suffolk his objective was primarily to fill the void left in the governance of the region by the execution of Edmund de la Pole in 1513. Brandon was expected to bind the local gentry more firmly to the new ruling dynasty and at the same time help frustrate the claims of Edmund's exiled brother Richard to both the duchy and the kingdom. The danger receded after Richard was killed at Pavia in Italy in 1525, and in the aftermath of the troubles of 1536 Henry ordered Brandon to reside in Lincolnshire permanently. There was some little delay while Katherine recovered from ague and their son Henry from smallpox, but they were back in the county by June 1537. The duke's lack of a substantial landed power-base there initially limited his authority, but the king gave him Tattershall Castle as his principal residence, and he acquired Lady Maria's dower third of the Willoughby properties (which included Grimsthorpe and Eresby) on her death in May 1539. With the Willoughby estates came a close network of local gentry supporters whose first loyalty was to Katherine and to Brandon as her husband.[10] She did not outrank him socially (as Mary Tudor had) and he assumed leadership of the 'connection' on her behalf.

We might suppose that Katherine was excited by the prospect of moving to Lincolnshire, but this is by no means certain. Many southerners (in the broadest sense of the word), regarded the inhabitants of the fenlands as uncouth and 'different', and we have already noted Henry VIII's description of them as the most 'brute and beastly' of his subjects.[11] The late fifteenth-century belief that rude and economically backward 'northerners' were looking for an excuse to rob and pillage in the wealthier south had not entirely dissipated, and Katherine may have felt that she was leaving the polite society of the court-orientated south-east for a place on the very edge of civilisation. But duty called, and duty had to be performed.

All the evidence suggests that by the late 1530s Brandon and Katherine were regarded as an exemplary couple and were on excellent terms with King Henry. Jane Seymour had given birth to a son, Edward, on 12 October 1537, and Brandon was invited to be one of the child's godfathers when he was baptised a week later. One source says that, when all was over, Katherine carried the infant back to his apartments followed by a 400-strong entourage, and she was again with the king and her husband when they attended a lavish banquet held at Hampton Court Palace in November 1538, a feast described by one guest as 'the best that ever I was at'.[12] At the same time she formed an attachment to the Princess Mary, playing cards and corresponding with her, and exchanging gifts. Mary had opposed her father's rejection of her mother and his religious changes, submitting only when threatened with dire consequences. She was now in her early twenties, and may have found Katherine's company a welcome distraction from the troubles of the recent past.

Queen Jane died of puerperal fever, or perhaps of a retained placenta, only twelve days after her son's birth, and the search for a new, fourth wife for Henry began almost immediately. At least nine European ladies were considered, and the choice fell on Anne, the twenty-four-year-old sister of the Duke of Cleves. Brandon and Katherine led the party that welcomed Anne to Dover at the end of December 1539, and Katherine became one of the six 'great ladies' of her household. But it all ended disastrously. Henry complained that his bride failed to excite him – which was another way of saying that he was becoming increasingly impotent – and they were divorced in July 1540. Brandon, who himself sired no more children after 1537, was instrumental in persuading Anne to accept the role of 'king's sister', and Cromwell, the principal architect of the union, paid with his head.

We noted that old Lady Willoughby's death in 1539 had helped Brandon establish himself in Lincolnshire, and it may have been significant for an entirely different reason. Throughout the 1530s Katherine had remained a staunch Roman Catholic – 'as earnest as any' in the opinion of the conservative Bishop of Winchester,

Stephen Gardiner – but in the next decade began to embrace evangelicalism, or Protestantism.[13] Gardiner recalled later that she had once been his 'gossip', a term typically used by godparents of their godchildren but also to imply close friendship, and it is likely that it was the removal of her mother's influence – and undoubted disapproval – that allowed her to change her views.

Stephen Gardiner was a Cambridge-educated canon lawyer who entered Cardinal Wolsey's service in 1524 and took a prominent part in negotiations with the papacy designed to resolve the king's 'Great Matter'. In 1529 he became Henry's principal secretary and his efforts were rewarded with promotion to the wealthy bishopric of Winchester two years later; but it was only with some difficulty that he accepted the king's decisions to divorce Queen Catherine without papal approval and make himself master of the Church in England. The more devoted Thomas Cromwell had replaced him as royal secretary by April 1534, but he partially regained Henry's goodwill by writing books defending the royal supremacy and the execution of Bishop Fisher. Privately, however, he hoped for reconciliation with Rome, and again managed to annoy the king by suggesting that he should make concessions to the leaders of the Pilgrimage of Grace. He remained out of favour until after Cromwell's execution in July 1540 when Henry sought his expertise in canon law to annul his marriage to Anne of Cleves and restored him to the Council. His position was again threatened when his nephew and secretary Germaine Gardiner was executed in 1544 on charges of denying the royal supremacy; but he continued to serve Henry on diplomatic missions and survived further reformist attempts to discredit him. He presumably only met, or noticed, Katherine after she became Duchess of Suffolk, and what had initially been an entirely cordial relationship soured as her religious stance altered. Matters were not improved when her friend John Dudley struck him in the face at a Council meeting in 1546.[14]

Katherine's conversion was to affect the rest of her life so profoundly that it seems appropriate to try to summarise what the differences between Catholics and Protestants really were. Today, we live in a generally tolerant society in which religion is (with some notable exceptions) essentially a private and personal matter; but this was not the case in the sixteenth century, when failure to conform was potentially as great an offence as committing treason. One of the main contrasts between the Tudor century and our own is that disagreements between the two faiths were often matters of life and death. Protestants desired a less elaborate, more direct, form of worship, one which did not require saints and priests to act as intermediaries. Accordingly, they saw no merit in undertaking pilgrimages to shrines, and believed that the 'Word of God' (the Bible) was an infinitely superior authority to the 'human traditions' of the papacy. They rejected transubstantiation, the Catholic belief that in the Eucharist the bread and wine became Christ's body and blood (the doctrine of the Real Presence), but adhered strongly to the concept of justification by faith. Catholics believed that salvation was attained by a combination of faith and (good) works, but the Protestant view was that it was a gift of God granted in return for faith and for faith alone.[15] Protestants denied the existence of purgatory, the idea that there was a kind of half-way house where sinners could do penance for their wrongdoing, and scorned the notion that the prayers of the living could determine whether a deceased went to heaven or hell. They also considered images of saints to be potentially idolatrous, and thought that Catholic devotion to the Virgin as Queen of Heaven diverted the faithful from the proper worship of Christ. The radical preacher Thomas Becon carried this view a step further, arguing that in the Bible 'such as ruled and were queens were for the most part wicked, superstitious, and given to idolatry and to all filthy abominations as we may see in the histories of Queen Jezebel'. Soon it was being said that women should not be allowed to govern in any circumstances, and John Knox's *First Blast of the Trumpet Against the Monstrous Regiment [Rule] of Women* held that feminine authority was unacceptable to God.

It is important to stress that these ideas developed over time, and that not all Protestants were as radical, or extreme, as others. Katherine's own spiritual journey began with the belief that scripture was the one authoritative guide to faith, and only later extended to a denial of transubstantiation and acceptance of justification by faith alone. Her correspondence shows that by the late 1540s she no longer believed in the physical presence of Christ in the Eucharist, and was wholly of the opinion that charitable acts could not expunge an individual's transgressions. She had long since ceased to use saints' days to date her letters, something Protestants avoided because of their opposition to the cult of saints and pilgrimages, and did her utmost to ensure that every parish in Lincolnshire had an English Bible. In the 1550s she embraced the doctrines of predestination and election, the beliefs that God 'ordered all things for the best' (even the most tragic events were part of His divine purpose), and that certain individuals, the 'elect', were guaranteed salvation. She became increasingly critical of clergy whose fondness for ornate robes and elaborate ritual (which the reformers associated with Catholicism) conflicted with her own preference for simple worship, and on one occasion dressed her dog, which she mockingly called Gardiner, in the white rochet, or vestment, of a bishop. In the early years she had to tread carefully – Henry VIII, for all his wrecking, never ceased to believe in transubstantiation and in the need for good works – but ultimately, this daughter of a Roman Catholic mother became one of the most fervent Protestants of her day.

What factors produced this dramatic – and ultimately uncompromising – change of heart? It can have had little to do with her husband, whose attitude to religion was as pragmatic and cautious as his approach to politics, and who did not lean towards either conservatives or reformers. 'Brandon's chaplains were more administrators, lawyers, teachers, and poets than preachers, [and] he held the middle ground out of an incalculable blend of mediocrity and cunning, at times, no doubt, even of confusion. He preserved an ambiguity which not even his clergy and officers – and quite possibly not even he himself – could penetrate.'[16] Unsurprisingly, he concurred with all his royal master's religious changes, and his willingness to temporise, to see both sides of an argument, made him popular with both Protestants and Catholics. When he and Katherine attended court they frequently came into contact with reformers like Edward Seymour, Earl of Hertford, the future Duke of Somerset, and John Dudley, Viscount Lisle, the future Earl of Northumberland, and were challenged by the arguments of the Protestant divine Hugh Latimer, who often preached before the king in the 1530s. When Augustine Bernher dedicated his sermons to Katherine in 1562, he recalled how God had used Latimer in 'Henry's days to be a singular instrument to set forth his truth, and by his preaching to open the eyes of such as were deluded by the subtle and deceitful crafts of the popish prelates'.[17]

Hugh Latimer was born at Thurcaston, in Leicestershire, some years before the turn of the century. The only son of yeoman farmers, his parents recognised his 'ready, prompt, and sharp wit' (Foxe) very early, and were prepared to invest some of their hard-earned wealth in his education. He went up to Cambridge at the age of fourteen, and was awarded the degrees of Bachelor of Arts (1511), Master of Arts (1514) and Bachelor of Theology (1524). His views in these early years were entirely conventional, and he used his examination sermon for his B.Th to denounce the teachings of Martin Luther's disciple Philip Melanchthon. Listening in the audience that day was the reformer Thomas Bilney, and he afterwards visited Latimer in his study. What happened next Latimer described in the first of the sermons on the Lord's Prayer he preached at Grimsthorpe in Katherine's presence many years later:

Here I have to tell you a story which happened at Cambridge. Master Bilney, or rather Saint Bilney, that suffered death for God's Word's sake [he was burnt in the Lollard's pit at Norwich in 1531], the same Bilney was the instrument whereby God called me to knowledge; for I may thank him, next to God, for that knowledge that I have in the Word of God. For I was as obstinate a papist as any was in England, insomuch that when I should be made bachelor of divinity, my whole oration went against Philip Melanchthon and against his opinions. Bilney heard me at that time, and perceived that I was zealous without knowledge; and he came to me afterwards in my study, and desired me, for God's sake, to hear his confession. I did so; and to say the truth, by his confession I learned more than before in many years. So from that time forward I began to smell the Word of God, and forsook the school doctors and such fooleries.[18]

The secrecy of the sacrament of confession allowed men like Bilney to voice 'heretical' opinions to fellow priests in complete confidence and he seized his opportunity – although Latimer's conversion to full-blown Protestantism was as gradual as Katherine's. As early as 1529 he advocated translating the Bible into English – something which was then illegal – but did not begin to seriously reappraise the Eucharist until the late 1540s. It was thanks to the patronage of Katherine's enemy, the reform-minded Queen Anne Boleyn, that he was invited to preach before the court from 1530 onwards and appointed Bishop of Worcester in 1535. His opinions were often at odds with Henry's[19] – his later sermons refer to narrow escapes that 'left his friends trembling in fear on his behalf' – and his situation became still more precarious after he voiced opposition to the king's Six Articles of Religion in 1539. Forced to resign his bishopric, he was imprisoned 'expecting every day to be led to execution'; and although he was released unharmed and granted a modest pension he was not allowed to preach again in Henry's lifetime. Anne Askew (discussed later) asked to see him after her condemnation, and he was again sent to the Tower under suspicion of heresy when the religious conservatives tried to undermine their opponents in the closing months of the reign.[20]

Latimer was perhaps the greatest influence on Katherine's religious thinking, but another seminal inspiration was Henry's sixth and last queen, Catherine Parr. The king had married his fifth wife, Catherine Howard, only three weeks after his divorce from Anne of Cleves, and had sent her to the block little more than a year later. The promiscuous teenager had wed Henry without disclosing her previous sexual experiences, and when it was discovered that she had held secret meetings with Thomas Culpeper, a gentleman of the king's privy chamber, after her marriage, contemporaries assumed the worst. The king and queen had stayed with Brandon and Katherine at Grimsthorpe in August 1541, and it was later said that this was one of the very few places on their tour 'where Catherine Howard had not misbehaved herself'.[21] Catherine may have been foolish rather than unfaithful, but Henry was sufficiently chastened by the experience to choose for his next wife a lady who was a decade older than her predecessor and a twice-married widow.[22] Katherine was one of only eighteen persons invited to attend the wedding, and it is likely that she and the new queen were already on terms of some intimacy. Catherine Parr was a committed Protestant, and admission to her circle may have helped crystallise thoughts which had been forming in Katherine Willoughby's mind for some years.

Prayer and Bible study were part of everyday life in Queen Catherine's household, and Katherine and her other ladies joined her in searching the scriptures and seeking a closer, personal relationship with God. Sermons preached by 'well learned and godly persons' stressed the authority of the Bible while emphasising the errors of Catholicism, and Queen Catherine composed a series of homilies entitled *Prayers Stirring the Mind unto Heavenly Meditations* in 1545. Thirty copies were distributed to her ladies and other reformers who used it to engage in what have been described as 'vigorous theological debates' on the doctrines of sin and salvation.[23] Many hours must have been passed in this manner, but again, not all Protestants would have approved of women taking such a leading role in expounding their faith.

Katherine's sojourn in Catherine Parr's household would have separated her from her home and family for long periods, but Charles Brandon knew better than anyone how much they owed to royal service. In April or May 1544 Katherine bade farewell to her now sixty-year-old husband when he embarked on what was to be his last military campaign in France. He distinguished himself at the siege of Boulogne, and Henry honoured him by inviting him to formally occupy the town after it surrendered on 14 September. He had spent the previous eight years buying up properties that complemented his and Katherine's Lincolnshire estate whenever he had the opportunity, and on his return was allowed to add the lands of Tattershall College to his portfolio of forfeited monastic assets for less than half their true value. Although still not fully in control of the county, he had achieved a position of dominance greater than he had formerly enjoyed in East Anglia, and had proclaimed his new wealth and authority by substantially rebuilding Grimsthorpe. The house has been much altered in the intervening centuries, but the southern and eastern fronts still incorporate much of his work.

Brandon remained in France until November 1544 and was apparently still reasonably active for a man of his years, but he died, quite suddenly, at Guildford, on 22 August 1545. He was widely respected and no doubt proud of his attractive wife and growing sons, but his later years were clouded by his relationship with his two daughters by Anne Browne and their husbands. Mary's spouse, Lord Monteagle, proved so impecunious that Brandon had to take over his lands and pay his debts on several occasions, and her sister Anne also needed money after Lord Powis obtained a legal separation on the grounds of her adultery. We know nothing of Katherine's relations with her two stepdaughters after Duchess Mary's funeral, and there is no record of them exchanging gifts or letters. They were both ten and more years her senior, and may have treated her with the coolness that children of a previous marriage often feel towards a younger, second wife.

Brandon had made his will during the siege of Boulogne on 24

August 1544. In it he asked to be buried in the collegiate church near Tattershall Castle, but his old friend King Henry insisted that he be interred in St George's Chapel, Windsor, at royal expense. Katherine regained full control of her own lands, and in accordance with standard practice was granted a dower third of her late husband's properties. Her eldest son Henry would inherit the remaining two-thirds when he came of age, and in the meantime she was able to buy his wardship and marriage from the Crown for £1,500 payable in seven instalments. Significantly, six of the seven courtiers who stood surety for her payment were prominent Protestants: Sir John Gates, Sir Philip Hoby, the king's physician George Owen, Sir Ralph Sadler, William Herbert, and Sir Anthony Denny. The seventh, Sir William Paget, had some evangelical sympathies, but his true religious views are less clear.

Brandon's executors were his 'entirely beloved wife', the Lord Chancellor Thomas Wriothesley, William Paulet Lord St John (another religious 'trimmer'), and Sir Anthony Browne, Anne Browne's half-brother and another long-standing friend of King Henry. He had assigned fifteen years' revenue from lands worth £620 a year to pay his debts, provide for his younger son Charles, and fund other legacies, and additionally, the generous sum of 8,000 marks (£5,333 6s 8d) was assigned to Charles to secure him an estate or, alternatively, to 'buy or obtain one gentlewoman having lands and tenements of inheritance' whom he would marry. Katherine, and Brandon's two daughters by Mary – Frances, Marchioness of Dorset, and Lady Eleanor Clifford – were left plate and jewels, but there was nothing for Lady Powis. Mary, Lady Monteagle, had died in 1544.

Katherine clearly enjoyed her husband's confidence, but there was one caveat. Brandon declared that she was to 'keep herself sole [single] and marry not after my death therewith' or she would lose her right to distribute the residue of his estate ('plate, jewels, household stuff, other goods and profits of land') in accordance with his wishes. His concern was that a second husband would persuade her to act in ways that were not in the heirs' best interests, but he need not have worried. She did not remarry until after her sons' deaths and in March 1546 the other executors allowed her to administer the bequests unsupervised because of the 'special trust and confidence that they bear towards [her]'. In a moment of blind perspicacity he asked the king to 'extend and continue his accustomed goodness towards my said entirely beloved wife, the Lady Katherine aforesaid'. He knew Henry liked her, but would have laughed at any suggestion that she might become his queen.[24]

Charles Wriothesley lamented the loss of Brandon, who 'had been so valiant a captain in the king's wars ... to the great damage and loss of the king's enemies', while Ellis Gruffyd commented that 'he was the flower of all the captains of the realm and had the necessary patience to control soldiers'.[25] They could have added that he was a competent administrator and an astute landlord, loyal to both his king and his family. The chronicler Edward Hall was in no doubt that he was 'a hardy [confident] gentleman and yet not too hardy, as almost of all estates and degrees of men high and low, rich and poor, heartily beloved',[26] and King Henry himself is said to have remarked that throughout his career he had never sought by word or deed to injure anyone. His early misalliances were a stain on his character and he was once (in 1515) accused of giving Sir William Compton 'a pain in the leg by sorcery',[27] but his behaviour in later years had been exemplary. There is no reason to doubt that Katherine and their sons mourned his passing, but she was twenty-six, wealthy, and attractive. The inexperienced and perhaps sometimes awkward teenager of the 1530s had become an accomplished young woman, one who could manage her household and extensive properties and take her place among the senior ladies of the kingdom. For many, the onset of widowhood marked the beginning of the end of life rather than a new opportunity, but for her, life had only just begun.

3

KING HENRY'S LAST LOVE
1545–1547

For the first time in her life Katherine was no longer subject to the authority of either her parents or her husband, and it is worth pausing to ask what sort of person she had become. A portrait painted at about this time shows an auburn-haired young woman wearing a black fur-trimmed gown and headdress with pleasant features and a slightly sad expression. In another likeness, produced a few years later in 1548, the black clothes are no longer decorated, she holds a prayer book, and her demeanour is more serious and confident. The change reflects both her passage into widowhood and her growing commitment to her Protestant faith.

Katherine was much admired by her Evangelical co-religionists, some of whose opinions bordered on hagiography. To the churchman and historian John Bale, writing in 1547, she was an example of those 'godly women' who were 'learned in the scriptures' and who bore comparison with 'such widows and wives as Paul, Peter and John commendeth in their epistles',[1] while John Parkhurst, who was briefly one of Charles Brandon's resident chaplains before transferring to Catherine Parr's household in

1543 and who in his spare time composed short Latin epitaphs and eulogies, almost ran out of superlatives:

> Aeternum salve, princeps clarissima mentis
> Dotibus, eximiis ad numeranda viris
> Vix dici poterit, quantum tribuat tibi vulgus,
> Quantum magnates, docta que turba virum.
> Nil tam suspiciunt homines tua stemmata clara
> Insignes dotes quam, Katharina tuos.

(Hail for ever, illustrious princess! The endowments of thy mind place thee on a level with men of the highest distinction. One can scarcely say how much all people – the common folk, nobility and men of learning alike – esteem thee, holding thee in high regard, O Katherine, not so much for thy glorious heritage as for thy singular talents.)[2]

Arguably, these reformist clergymen were bound to think highly of someone in authority who shared their opinions, but they were not alone. In March 1537 Honor, Lady Lisle, the wife of the deputy of Calais, was seeking to place Anne and Katherine Bassett, the daughters of her first marriage, in great households, and John Husee, her confidential agent in England, arranged for Sir William Coffin, a knight of the king's privy chamber, to approach Katherine Willoughby. Katherine indicated her willingness to accept Katherine Bassett, and Husee was sure that, with careful handling, the matter would be brought to a satisfactory conclusion:

And touching the suit to be made for Mrs [sic] Katherine [Bassett], I trust the same be now at a good stay, for your ladyship [Honor Lisle] shall understand that Mr [sic] Coffin hath moved the Duchess of Suffolk of it, and hath so handled the matter that her Grace hath made him grant thereof, so that he willed me to write to your ladyship in it. And now, since, it is chanced that there is one dead in my Lord of Suffolk's house, so that neither he ne my Lady shall for a time come to the Court. But in the meantime [he continues in his rather laboured style] Mr Coffin thinketh that it should be well done that your ladyship and my Lord [Lisle] both did write so gentle letters unto my Lady Suffolk, declaring by the same how that you have had knowledge that by Mr Coffin's suit her Grace hath vouchsafed to accept your ladyship's daughter to her service, for the which my lord and your ladyship doth render her most entire thanks, and trusteth that she shall do her Grace good service; and also how that your ladyship hath heard that there is one dead in my lord's house, by reason whereof her Grace doth absent herself from the Court for a time, which notwithstanding, your ladyship desireth to know her pleasure when you shall send your said daughter. And this Mr Coffin thinketh best and that she shall be so much the better received.[3]

Honor Lisle expressed some reservations, perhaps because Katherine Willoughby was only just eighteen in March 1537, although Husee assured his mistress that she was 'virtuous, wise and discreet'.[4] He was still trying to persuade her in October when he remarked that 'as for Mrs Katherine [Bassett], my Lady Sussex and my Lady Rutland saith that your ladyship cannot better bestow her than with my Lady Suffolk',[5] but Honor may not have been entirely responsible for the plan's failure. It seems that Katherine Willoughby was one of life's procrastinators, someone who put things off from day to day, from week to week, and ultimately, from month to month, without weighing the effect on those who were expecting a response from her. Two years later, in 1539, the Lisles again tried to cultivate the Brandons, although this time the reason is uncertain. Husee says only that 'touching my Lady Suffolk, I have written her Grace according to your ladyship's [Honor's] pleasure, and am promised shortly to have an answer',[6] but if he thought that the gift of a spaniel sent to Katherine in February would bring a swift and positive outcome he was mistaken. In letter after letter he informs Honor that 'as yet I hear nothing from my Lady Suffolk's grace', and 'my Lady Suffolk's answer is not yet come, whereat I do marvel',[7] and although the Brandons were grateful for a quantity of wine the Lisles sent them in June, they did not, apparently, thank them personally.[8] About 22 June Husee approached Brandon who told him that 'the duchess's grace, his wife, was now in Lincolnshire and that his Grace [Brandon] was riding thitherward; and that at his Grace's coming thither he would consult with her Grace, and thereupon to make your ladyship [Honor] such an answer as you should be pleased withal',[9] but again, nothing happened. Finally, Brandon's man, Francis Hall, was asked to use his good offices, and on 29 August he was able to tell Honor that he was forwarding a letter from his mistress 'written with her own hand after midnight at Sheffield Castle in Hallamshire, as I shall tell you more at leisure at our next meeting with the grace of God'.[10] As is often the case with belated thanks, Katherine's were fulsome and included several expressions of friendship, but there is no mention of Honor's suit:

Madam, In my most hearty wise I heartily recommend me unto your ladyship, heartily thank you for your good wine you sent me, which I ensure you was very good. And also, I heartily thank you for your little dog you sent me, wherein I promise you you have done me no little pleasure, which I promise you I shall be glad to acquit whenever it shall lie in me to do you any pleasure, to be as ready to it as any friend you have. Madam, my lord, my husband has him heartily recommended to you and to my lord your husband, and thanks you both for your kindness. Also I pray you to have me heartily recommended to my lord your husband as she which would be glad to be acquainted with him. No more to you at this time, but I beseech Jesu have you in his keeping. Written at my Lord of Shrewsbury's house in Yorkshire, the Saturday after our Lady Day the Assumption. By your assured friend to my power, Katherine Suffolk.[11]

But dilatoriness was not Katherine's only failing. She herself admitted that her temper was often short and her tongue sharp, and there were occasions when even her friends thought it prudent to take cover. Richard Morrison, the English ambassador to the court of Charles V, remarked on her 'heats', regretting that 'so goodly a wit waiteth on so froward a will', and on another occasion she had to apologise to William Cecil for her 'foolish choler' and 'brawling', begging his 'forgiveness on my knees'. Hugh Latimer said pointedly that some women 'should keep their tongues in better order' in one of the sermons he preached before her at Grimsthorpe, and if he was not immune from her rages then neither (presumably) were members of her household and servants.[12] Katherine Bassett may not have been altogether sorry that things had turned out the way they had.

A hasty word, a flash of anger on the spur of the moment, was one thing, but there were also times when Katherine went out of her way to cause ill feeling. John Foxe tells of an occasion in her husband's lifetime when they hosted a dinner at which Bishop Stephen Gardiner was one of the guests. Charles Brandon suggested that each lady present should invite the gentleman she 'loved best' to take her into dinner, whereupon Katherine took Gardiner by the hand saying that 'forasmuch as she could not sit down with my lord whom she loved best (Brandon had apparently ruled himself out of contention), she had chosen him whom she loved worst'.[13] It was one thing to dress her dog in a white rochet and name it 'Gardiner', but this was a direct, personal insult inflicted in the presence of other members of aristocratic society. Clearly, she did not think that as the hostess it behoved her to be polite to everyone, and the incident must be seen as part of an unfortunate, and growing, tendency to be contemptuous of those she disagreed with. Regrettably, Foxe does not tell us what her husband thought of her behaviour, or what he said to her after their guests had gone home!

The person who emerges from these incidents is self-assured, but prone to anger and forthright or dismissive to the point of rudeness. She was in no doubt that, in matters of religion, she was right (and those who disagreed with her were therefore wrong), and we may wonder if her rather offhand treatment of Honor Lisle was not unconnected to her own nascent Protestantism and Honor's staunch Catholicism. Later on, she would display great loyalty to her friends and a remarkable stoicism in adversity, although she can never have been 'easy' to deal with. She did admit her faults, however, and without them would not have been the woman she was.

We noted earlier that it was Katherine's mother's death which first allowed her to indulge her taste for Protestantism, and her admission into Catherine Parr's circle and the removal of her husband's restraining hand combined to accelerate the process. She forged closer relationships with the leading reformers, not least Edward Seymour, to whom she gave a horse in the spring of 1544, and John Dudley, to whose infant daughter she stood godmother in November 1545. Although it was only three months since Charles Brandon's death Katherine made her London home available to those invited to attend the ceremony, and, for a short period, laid her formal mourning aside. At the beginning of 1547 Chapuys confided to Mary of Hungary that 'the King of England gives his countenance to his stirrers-up of heresy, the Earl of Hertford [Seymour] and the Lord Admiral [Dudley], which may be feared … because, according to report, the queen, instigated thereto by the Duchess of Suffolk [Katherine], the Countess of Hertford, and the admiral's wife, is infected by the sect, which she would not be likely to favour, at least openly, unless she knew the king's feeling'.[14] Conservatives were becoming alarmed by the pace of change, and feared what might happen when the ailing king died.

Chapuys had left London in 1545, and may not have been aware of a story which his successor as Imperial ambassador, François Van der Delft, reported to Charles V in February 1546. 'Sire, I am confused and apprehensive to inform your majesty,' he began apologetically,

> that there are rumours here of a new queen, although I do not know why, or how true it may be. Some people attribute it to the sterility of the present queen, whilst others say that there will be no change whilst the present war [with France] lasts. Madame Suffolk [Katherine] is much talked about, and is in great favour; but the king shows no alteration in his demeanour towards the queen,

though the latter, as I am informed, is somewhat annoyed at the rumours.[15]

The speculation had reached Europe by early March when Stephen Vaughan, the king's factor in Antwerp, advised Thomas Wriothesley and William Paget that

> this day came to my lodging a High Dutch, a merchant of this town, saying that he had dined with certain friends, one of whom offered to lay a wager with him that the King's Majesty would have another wife; and he prayed me to show him the truth. He would not tell me who offered the wager, and I said that I never heard of any such thing, and that there was no such thing. Many folks talk of this matter, and from whence it comes I cannot learn.[16]

Rumours are sometimes without foundation, but there are strong indications that King Henry found Katherine attractive. They had been exchanging New Year gifts since 1534, and Chapuys noted that he had been 'masking and visiting' with her in March 1538, only months after Jane Seymour's death. 'The king,' he wrote, 'has been in much better humour than ever he was, making musicians play on their instruments all day along. He went to dine at a splendid house of his, where he had collected all his musicians, and, after giving orders for the erection of certain sumptuous buildings therein, returned home by water, surrounded by musicians, and went straight to visit the Duchess of Suffolk ... and ever since cannot be one single moment without masks.'[17] Henry might have wed her then had she been single, and the disappointments of his later marriages can only have enhanced his feelings towards her. It is possible that by 1546 he had grown impatient with Queen

Catherine's failure to give him a second son, and more than ever saw this younger, perhaps more attractive, woman who was now a widow and the mother of two healthy boys as the solution to his problem. He would not have been the first man to think that a new, more exciting, relationship would somehow restore his lost youth.

The real question, of course, is, had Henry and Katherine already become lovers, perhaps in the late 1530s or thereafter? And had Charles Brandon, the courtier par excellence, turned a diplomatically blind eye? The answer will probably always elude us, but William Carey had long tolerated the king's liaison with his wife, Mary Boleyn, and both he and Brandon would have been anxious to retain the irascible monarch's favour. Carey received substantial grants between 1522 and 1525 when Mary was Henry's mistress, presumably as a reward for his understanding, and it could have been for the same reason that twenty years later Brandon was allowed to buy Tattershall College on the generous terms already noticed.[18] Katherine had waited on both Anne of Cleves and Catherine Howard before joining Catherine Parr's household, and in this capacity would have been regularly at court and 'available' to Henry. And what Henry wanted, he usually got.

We catch only occasional glimpses of Katherine during her years of attendance on the king's fourth and fifth wives, but there was one occasion when both his present and former spouses and (we suppose) his mistress all enjoyed an amicable time together. On 3 January 1541 Anne of Cleves came to Hampton Court to present her New Year gifts, a handsome pair of horses caparisoned in mauve velvet, to Henry and Catherine Howard in person, and, we are informed, was received by the duchess of Suffolk [Katherine], the countess of Hertford, and certain other ladies, who, after conducting her to the rooms destined for her lodging, took her to the queen's apartments. Having entered the room, Lady Anne approached the queen with as much reverence and punctilious ceremony as if she herself were the most insignificant damsel about court, all the time addressing the queen on her knees, notwithstanding the prayers and entreaties of the latter, who received her most kindly, showing her great favour and courtesy. At this time the king entered the room, and, after making a very low bow to Lady Anne, embraced and kissed her, upon which he and his queen sat down to supper in their usual places, whilst their visitor was made to occupy a seat near the bottom of the table, all the time keeping as good a mien and countenance, and looking as unconcerned as if there had been nothing between them. After supper all three conversed for a while in the most gracious manner, and when the king retired to his own apartments, the queen and Lady Anne first danced together ...[19]

It is hard to believe that any of these women genuinely liked one another, but appearances had to be maintained.

Now, five years later, Henry had another Catherine, and the religious conservatives were quick to seize their opportunity when they sensed that his feelings towards her had cooled. Their first victim was Anne Askew, a Lincolnshire gentlewoman who had rejected an unhappy arranged marriage, turned to religion, and become an outspoken Protestant. Her sister was married to a lawyer in Katherine's household, and the Catholic author Robert Parsons alleged that Katherine arranged meetings between Askew and Queen Catherine before the former was arrested in April

1546. Her opinions were so far removed from the royal view of what constituted orthodoxy that they could easily be construed as subversive, and her interrogators hoped that she would confirm that the queen and other reformers shared them. Katherine and her friends must have been concerned by what Askew would say about them under torture, but no amount of racking could persuade her to implicate her contacts. The most she would admit was that two men acting on behalf of the Countess of Hertford and Lady Denny had given her money, and Katherine must have been saddened and not a little frustrated by her inability to help her when she was burned at the stake in July.

It is not always easy in these days of 'take it or leave it' religion to appreciate the fervour, the degree of commitment felt by women like Katherine and Anne Askew. Askew's account of her ordeal is written in almost matter-of-fact language without a trace of self-pity, and the reader can only try to imagine how much she suffered for what was after all only a belief, an alternative interpretation of scripture. Before her execution she told how

> they did put me on the rack, because I confessed no ladies or gentlewomen to be of my opinion, and thereon they kept me a long time; and because I lay still, and did not cry, my lord chancellor [Thomas Wriothesley] and Master Rich took pains to rack me with their own hands till I was nigh dead. Then the lieutenant [of the Tower] caused me to be loosed from the rack. Incontinently, I swooned, and then they recovered me again. After that I sat two long hours reasoning with my lord chancellor upon the bare floor; where he, with many flattering words, persuaded me to leave my opinion. But my Lord God (I thank his everlasting goodness) gave me grace to persevere, and will do, I hope, to the very end.[20]

The torture of a gentlewoman, especially one who had already been condemned, was unprecedented, and the personal involvement of Wriothesley and Richard Rich, Wriothesley's successor as chancellor, shows that this was no ordinary interrogation. The conservatives were determined to hunt down their opponents, and in this febrile charged climate no one – not even the Duchess of Suffolk – could feel entirely safe.

Askew's determined silence had thwarted Bishop Gardiner and his cronies for the moment, but not for long. King Henry may have blamed Queen Catherine for failing to give him a son, but Foxe believed that another reason for their deteriorating relationship was her readiness to challenge her husband's opinions when they discussed matters of religion. Henry, who thought himself no mean theologian, is said to have wearied of these arguments – perhaps he did not always win them – and was heard to complain that 'a good hearing it is when women become such clerks; and a thing much to my comfort, to come in mine old days to be taught by my wife'. Gardiner, who was present, replied that, in his opinion, 'the religion by the queen, so stiffly maintained, [which] did disallow and dissolve the policy and politic government of princes' merited death under the laws of the kingdom, and offered to obtain further evidence that would disclose this 'treason cloaked with the cloak of heresy'. His intention was to search the closets of some of Catherine's ladies for heretical books and other incriminating material, and then have the queen arrested and sent to the Tower.

It seemed that this time, there was no escape for Catherine and her ladies, but their enemies were again foiled. Henry confided his intentions to Doctor Wendy, one of his physicians, and the bill of articles against Catherine was dropped by an unnamed councillor, found by one of her friends, and brought to her. Realising she was in mortal danger, she 'fell incontinent into a great melancholy and agony, bewailing and taking on in such sort as was lamentable to see', and Dr Wendy, who was summoned to attend her, advised her to 'show her humble submission unto the king' who he was sure would be 'gracious and favourable' to her. Henry, hearing of her sudden illness, visited her and offered words of reassurance, but she did not allow herself to be lulled into a false sense of security. She immediately ordered her ladies to dispose of their reformist books (she had earlier entrusted her own to her uncle, Lord Parr of Horton), and the following evening went to her husband's chamber where she found him talking with several of his gentlemen. Henry turned the conversation to religion appearing to desire her opinion, and she, seizing her opportunity, begged him to excuse her 'your majesty being so excellent in gifts and ornaments of wisdom, and I a silly poor woman, so much inferior in all respects of nature to you'. She explained that she had never tried to instruct him, but

whereas I have, with your majesty's leave, heretofore been bold to hold talk with your majesty, wherein sometimes in opinions there has seemed some difference, I have not done it so much to maintain opinion, as I did it rather to minister talk, not only to the end your majesty might with less grief pass over this painful time of your infirmity, being attentive to our talk, and hoping that your majesty should reap some ease thereby; but also that I, hearing your majesty's learned discourse, might receive to myself some profit thereby.

Henry was mollified by this combination of self-abasement and flattery, and embraced her with the words, 'And is it even so, sweet heart? And tended your arguments to no worse end? Then perfect friends we are now again, as ever at any time heretofore.'[21]

Unfortunately, no one told Lord Chancellor Wriothesley that the situation had altered, and when he came with an armed escort to arrest Catherine he found her walking with her husband in the garden. He was sent packing with Henry's curses ringing in his ears.

The whole incident, as related by Foxe, had been a close call for the queen and her Protestant circle, but there are indications that King Henry never meant to allow the conservatives an outright victory. By forewarning Dr Wendy and, we may suppose, allowing the bill of articles to be 'lost' where someone close to Catherine could find it, he was giving her an opportunity to redeem herself; and it seems likely that Wriothesley was not told of their reconciliation so that he and his associates could be put firmly in their collective place. The idea that Henry was toying with his wife and his ministers, playing them off against one another in order to assert his own authority, may seem improbable at first glance, but the only logical conclusion is that Catherine Parr – unlike Anne Boleyn and Catherine Howard – was effectively being given a second chance. Far from gaining the ascendency over his opponents, Gardiner was not named among the councillors who would govern for Prince Edward after the king's death, and another of his allies, the Duke of Norfolk, was spared only because Henry died the night before he was due to be executed – for not informing against his son Henry Howard, Earl of Surrey, who had stupidly flaunted his Plantagenet ancestry by quartering the royal arms with his own. Henry Howard had defended himself brilliantly at his trial, and was only condemned after the king's opinion had been sought and the jurors 'interviewed'. Henry could still overawe his subjects, and never lost his grip on the levers of power.

Those who remained close to the king in this last phase of his life must have felt that they were treading eggshells and could be arrested at any moment for the most innocent of deeds or comments. Perhaps the fundamental problem was that Henry's religious revolution had gone further than he had originally intended and he feared that he was losing – or had lost – control of it. An autocratic king might grant his people certain liberties, but always on the implied understanding that they were a concession which remained subject to his approval and which could be withdrawn at any moment. The 'people' could never be allowed to take liberties or to set the agenda, and the outwardly capricious, often deadly game Henry was playing had in reality a very clear objective. He wanted unity and he demanded obedience; and any who overlooked this would soon feel his wrath.

The question we must try to answer, of course, is of just how close Katherine Willoughby came to becoming King Henry's seventh wife and queen. The evidence is slight and tantalisingly inconclusive, but there can be no doubt that she was on familiar terms with him and that the possibility of marrying her did enter his calculations. But perhaps, in the end, even Henry had to face the reality that he would have no more children – by his present wife or any other – and what had begun as a serious proposition became a game in which he toyed with some of his leading subjects' emotions. The reality is that he would have found Katherine's forceful Protestantism as disconcerting as Queen Catherine's if he had allowed her to take Catherine's position, and it made no sense to exchange one virago for another. The feistiness he admired in her as a subject could have made her less appealing as a wife.

Katherine, for her part, could hardly have refused a proposal from her own sovereign, but other evidence suggests that she was in no hurry to remarry. Lady Cecilie Goff mentions a tradition that when the Polish ambassador failed to obtain the hand of the Princess Mary for his master King Sigismund, he paid court to

Katherine; and Van der Delft thought that she was about to wed Lord Hertford's brother Thomas Seymour at the beginning of May 1547.[22] The Polish ambassador's interest is feasible – he may well have considered other ladies after being denied Princess Mary – but Van der Delft was probably confusing his Catherines. It can hardly be coincidence that Thomas Seymour married the by then widowed Catherine Parr – with Katherine Willoughby's blessing – towards the end of the same month.[23]

Henry's health began to worsen in 1546, although it was perhaps never as bad as some have suggested. He made his customary autumn progress only six months before he died, and to the end signed warrants and read and noted dispatches. He had become extremely large and needed mechanical devices to help him mount and ascend stairs; but there is no evidence that he was unable to pass through doors or that the efforts of several servants were required to literally wheel him from room to room. He was never the 'mass of loathsome infirmities' described by one writer, although it is likely that his ulcerated leg and high blood pressure – aggravated by the diet and remedies of the period – did nothing to improve his temper. He died on 28 January 1547, and Katherine, we must assume, took her place among the queen's ladies at his magnificent funeral procession, which lasted from 14 to 16 February. Perversely, this great reformer, who had done so much to damage traditional Catholicism in England, desired that Masses be said for his soul 'so long as the world shall endure', and ensured that the heraldic displays which formed an essential part of the proceedings acknowledged only two queens, Jane Seymour and Catherine Parr. Katherine of Suffolk may have reflected that marrying a king like Henry was a dangerous undertaking, and felt relief tinged with disappointment that she had not had to tread that path.

4

TRAGEDY
1547–1553

King Henry's death and his son Edward's accession heralded a new dawn for Katherine and those of her religious persuasion. In his last years the king, fearing that his restructuring of the Church had gone too far, had reaffirmed some of the traditional tenets of Catholicism; but his son was a Protestant reformer after Katherine's own heart. Quite how Henry had allowed Edward to be brought up in a tradition alien to his own is something of a mystery. The main 'culprits' were his tutors, Richard Cox and John Cheke, two of the best qualified teachers of their day, perhaps best described as 'closet Protestants'. Catherine Parr knew of their reformist sympathies (she once referred to them as 'Christ's special advocates'), but they had publically deferred to Henry in matters of religion while he lived. Katherine Willoughby would look back on Edward's short reign as a golden era, but it was an era tainted with tragedy nearer home.

The king had made provision for his ten-year-old son's guidance and government in the will he drew up in the closing weeks of his life. His sixteen executors would constitute a Council of Regency, while twelve others would be available to offer advice 'when they or any of them shall be called'. No one individual was to have pre-eminence over the others, and all decisions were to be taken by a majority vote. Bishop Gardiner was excluded – Henry thought him 'so stubborn ... that no man would be able to control him' – but the king failed to appreciate that some of the reformers he nominated were no less ambitious. One clause in the will – inserted, possibly, when he was no longer able to comprehend it and signed with his dry stamp – charged the executors to satisfy any promises relating to gifts or promotions which remained unfulfilled when he died.[1] Its effect was to allow the councillors to award themselves whatever titles and grants of land they claimed they were about to be given, and Edward Seymour, Lord Hertford, made a mockery of Henry's intentions when he secured his appointment as Lord Protector and Duke of Somerset. The earldoms of Warwick and Southampton bought the compliance of John Dudley and the conservative Thomas Wriothesley, William Parr (Queen Catherine's brother) became Marquis of Northampton, and there were peerages for Richard Rich, Thomas Seymour, and Katherine's cousin William (her uncle Sir Christopher's son), among others.

The coronation was fixed for Sunday 20 February, and Edward made his formal procession from the Tower to Westminster the previous day. A good number of young aristocrats were traditionally admitted to the order of the Bath on these occasions, and Katherine's two sons, Henry, titular Duke of Suffolk, who was now aged eleven, and Charles, ten, were among the forty who kept vigil throughout Friday night before receiving their knightly swords and spurs from the king the following morning. The coronation ceremony and the banquet which followed it would normally have lasted for some twelve hours, but this was reduced to around seven so as not to unduly weary Edward. It may also have come as a relief to young Henry Brandon, whose principal duty that day was to carry the orb.

Katherine was no doubt delighted that her Protestant friends had gained the ascendancy, but she may not have appreciated that routing their opponents would allow them to quarrel among themselves. Thomas Seymour was jealous that Somerset, his elder brother, had taken control of both the king and the government, and tried to persuade Edward to appoint him his personal governor. Edward decided – or was advised – not to take such a step, but Seymour proceeded to cultivate the support of other noblemen and began to pay court to Princess Elizabeth although he had only recently married Queen Catherine. Catherine died after giving birth to a daughter, Mary, on 30 August 1548, and although Seymour redoubled his efforts to charm Edward and wed Elizabeth he made little headway. His frustration finally boiled over when, on the night of the 16 January following (if we may entirely believe the Spanish ambassador's account of what happened), he tried to kidnap the king only to be thwarted by Edward's pet dog, whose barking roused the guards. It was a mad, desperate scheme – what he really hoped to achieve by it is unfathomable – and inevitably, he paid with his head.

Katherine had returned to Grimsthorpe with her sons after the coronation ceremonies were over, and it was here that she learned of Catherine Parr's death and of Seymour's bizarre plot to gain control of Edward. In the last year of the queen's life Katherine had encouraged her to publish her exposition of her own religious beliefs and experience, and this appeared as *The Lamentations of a Sinner* in November 1547. It had a flattering preface by William Cecil, who was at this time a member of the Duke of Somerset's household, and Katherine undoubtedly took pleasure in helping to promote it. In one of her letters to Thomas Seymour the queen remarked that 'as my Lady of Suffolk saith, God is a marvellous man', and their mutual admiration had doubtless fostered their commitment to the reformed faith.[2]

But while Katherine was always happy to encourage the queen's interest in religious matters, she proved decidedly less willing to provide for her late friend's orphaned baby daughter. One of Thomas Seymour's dying wishes was that little Mary should be brought up at Grimsthorpe, and she duly arrived there accompanied by her governess, Elizabeth Aglionby, a nurse, two maids, and other servants. The Duke of Somerset had led Katherine to believe that she would receive an allowance from the girl's father's confiscated properties to pay for her upkeep, but time passed and none was forthcoming. William Parr declined to share the responsibility in these circumstances, and in July she asked Cecil to use his influence to help her while being careful not to betray her request:

I have so wearied myself with the letters that I have written at this present to my Lord's Grace and to my Lady [the Duke and Duchess of Somerset], that there is not so much as one line could be spared for Cecil. But by that time I have made you the amends, you will be well pleased by another line; you shall have letters when they get none, That is to say, I will trouble you when I will not trouble them. So I trow you may hold you well repaid. In these my letters to my Lady, I do put her in remembrance for the performance of the promise touching some annual pension for the finding of the late queen's child; for now she with a dozen persons lyeth all together at my charge, the continuance whereof will not bring me out of debt this year. My Lord Marquis Northampton, to whom I [page torn] deliver her, hath as weak a back for such a burden as I have. And he would receive her but more willingly if he might receive her with the appurtenances [property]. Thus groweth matters; you must help us beggars and I pray that you may. And then we will cease our importunities. But never a word that you are required by me. So fare you well, with my commendations to your wife.[3]

Katherine's hope was that the Duchess of Somerset would choose an appropriate moment to remind her busy husband of his obligation to little Mary, but still nothing happened. A few weeks later she again wrote to Cecil, describing her troubles as a 'sickness' which 'increaseth mightily upon me', not least because 'the queen's child hath layen, and still doth lie at my house, with her company about her, wholly at my charges'. She then informs him,

I have written to my Lady of Somerset at large [again?], that there be some pension allotted unto her [Mary] according to my Lord Grace's promise. Now, good Cecil, help at a pinch all that you may help. My Lady also sent me word at Whitsuntide, by Bertie [Richard Bertie, Katherine's gentleman usher], that my Lord's Grace, at her suit, had also granted [that] certain nursery plate should be delivered with the child. And lest there might be stay [delay] for lack of a present bill for such plate and stuff as there was in the nursery, I send you here enclosed of all such parcels as were appointed for the child's only use, and that you may the better understand that I cry not before I am pricked. I send you also Mrs Aglionby's letter unto me, who with the maid's nurse and others, daily call one for their wages, whose voices my ears hardly bear, but my coffers much worse. Wherefore I cease, and commit me and my sickness to your diligent cure with my hearty commendations to your wife.

At my manor of Grimsthorpe, your assured loving friend, K. Suffolk.[4]

The list of 'plate and stuff' Katherine enclosed with her letter has survived, and is an interesting record of what was deemed necessary for a highborn infant at this period:

First:

    2 pots of silver all white

    3 goblets of silver all white

    1 salt, silver and parcel gilt

    A 'muster' with a band of silver and parcel gilt

    11 spoons all white

Item: A quilt for the cradle, 3 pillows, and 1 pair of fustians

Item: 3 feather beds, 3 quilts, and 3 pairs of fustians

Item: A tester of scarlet, embroidered, with a counterpoint of sail saye belonging to the same, and curtains of crimson taffeta

Item: 2 counterpoints of imagery for the nurse's bed

Item: 6 pairs of sheets of little worth

Item: 6 fair pieces of hangings within the inner chamber

Item: 4 carpets for the windows

Item: 10 pieces of hangings of the twelve months within the outer chamber

Item: 2 cushions of cloth of gold

Item: 1 chair of cloth of gold

Item: 2 wrought stools

Item: A bedstead gilt, with a tester, and counterpoint with curtains belonging to same

Item: 2 'mellche beastes' which were belonging to the nursery, the which it may please your Grace to write may be bestowed upon the two maids towards their marriage, which shall be shortly.

Item: 1 lute

Endorsed: To my loving friend, Mr Cecil, attendant upon my Lord Protector's Grace.[5]

Lady Goff says that Mary eventually married Sir Edward Bushel, a gentleman in attendance on James I's wife Anne of Denmark, but this must be thought highly improbable. Anne did not marry James until 1589, by which time Mary would have been forty-one, and the clergyman-historian John Strype (1643–1737) thought she had died in infancy. Strype was perhaps better informed than we are, and her death would explain Katherine's subsequent silence on the matter. She would surely have mentioned the girl in her later correspondence with Cecil if she had continued to reside with her, whether funds were provided or not.

But was Katherine really embarrassed financially by the needs of a baby and a few servants, or was it more a case of not allowing others to shift the burden? Her late husband's debts and the acquisition of her eldest son's wardship must have drained her resources, but in May 1546 she was granted a licence to retain forty persons in her livery besides household servants, and had no fewer than 'ninety horses and geldings of all ages ... and thirty-five mares' in her stables and pastures at Grimsthorpe.[6] These figures hardly imply financial stringency, and there is no hint of economy in 'an inventory of apparel and other things lent by the duchess to her sons, the Duke of Suffolk and Lord Charles Brandon, and bought by her' drawn up five years later.

In the list of articles lent to the Duke of Suffolk are – A black velvet gown furred with sables and 'guarded with two passamour laces'; a pair of crimson velvet hose with nether stocks of crimson silk; a nightgown of black damask, furred with conie; a velvet cap with fourteen diamonds; another velvet cap with fourteen rubies; a diamond set in gold; a 'tallet' with four emeralds; buttons of pearl set in gold, a dial of bone, nine racketts and two rings 'for the tylte'.

Amongst Lord Charles Brandon's things are – a suit of crimson satin embroidered with silver, given to the Duchess by the King, with buttons of gold; a night gown of grogram furred with jennet; a cape with seventeen pair of 'agletts' and sixteen buttons; and a taffeta hat with a broach.[7]

Unfortunately we have no record of how much all these items cost, nor of the extent to which Katherine's income covered – or failed to cover – her outgoings. But it is not without interest that when Sir William Sharington was arrested in January 1549 the inventory of goods and valuables found in his possession included 'jewels of [the Duchess of] Suffolk, of great value', left with him 'for assurance of £11,000'. That funds were sometimes in short supply is indicated by her promise, made in December of that year, that 'Dr Cornelius 'shall have his money in a fortnight, or a little and [the rest?] later', and there are hints that her properties were not always managed efficiently. Part of a letter she wrote to Cecil in October 1550 indicates that she had turned to commerce to help satisfy her ever pressing need for cash:

I am content to become your partner as you promise me, and I will abide all adventures in your ship, be the weather fair or foul; and though I cannot help you with costly wares to furnish her, yet I shall ply you with my woollen stuffs which may serve her for ballast.

If you marvel how that I am become so cunning in ship works, you shall understand that I am about the making of one here by me at Boston, or rather the passing of an old one; which gentle recompense I had for my wines herewith the *Honor* victualled the rebels in Norfolk last year; so that I am now become a merchant vintner. Thus, many ways, beggars seek their thrift; which having sought, I cannot find by land, and mind now to try my luck by water: and if I speed well, I promise you as liberally to divide with you as you promise me.

Not every aristocratic family would have thought it appropriate to turn to 'trade', but Katherine, whose father had been allowed to deal in wool and to export malt and fifty tons of beer annually from Boston, had no such scruples. Caring for Mary would have been an additional, unwanted burden if she was overspent and already borrowing heavily, but the cost would have represented only a small part of the total upkeep of the whole establishment. The implication is that Katherine would go to any lengths to maintain appearances, but that caring for another's child – even the child of a close friend – was quite another matter. In another of her letters to Cecil she again remarked that 'all the world knoweth … what a very *beggar* I am'.[8] But beggars are not all of one sort.

Unsurprisingly perhaps, Katherine used the new political and religious climate to promote the cause of Protestantism within Lincolnshire. John Strype remarked that the reformed faith was greatly advanced 'by the helping forwardness of that devout woman of God, the Duchess of Suffolk', and added that

she was very active in seconding the efforts of government to abolish superfluous Holy Days, to remove images and relics from the churches, to destroy shrines and other monuments of idolatry and superstition, to put an end to pilgrimages, to reform the clergy, to see that every church had provided, in some convenient place, a copy of the large Bible, to stir up the bishops, vicars and curates to diligence in preaching against the usurped authority of the Pope; in inculcating upon all the reading of the Scriptures, and especially the young, the Pater Noster, the Articles of Faith, and the Ten Commandments in English.[9]

It is clear that Katherine was very much a 'hands-on' reformer, who later would risk royal displeasure by sending money to the imprisoned Bishop Ridley and by forwarding his tracts and letters to her Protestant friends Joan Wilkinson and Anne Warcup. She shared the 'heretical' books she kept in her library with others, and helped the Protestant Dutch and French congregations in London obtain permission to worship according to their own rituals in their own newly acquired church. After her husband's death in 1545 she increasingly promoted evangelicals to the livings under her authority, and six years later used chantry land she acquired at Spilsby to found a grammar school – with the proviso that she and her heirs would have the right to choose the (Protestant) schoolmaster. It was not for nothing that Thomas Some and Augustine Bernher dedicated their collections of Latimer's sermons to her, or that John Day and other reformist printers decorated their publications with her coat of arms.

But Katherine did not always see eye to eye with her co-religionists. She criticised reformers who schemed to cause trouble for one another, and (as we will see) decried parents who arranged marriages for their children for financial or political reasons without considering their future happiness.[10] Her old adversary Bishop Gardiner had been committed to the Tower in the summer of 1549 for his continuing opposition to the government's religious changes, and one day when Katherine was in London she saw him looking out from a window of his prison. According to Foxe the bishop saluted her by doffing his bonnet, but she rejected the gesture with the words 'that it is merry with the lambs now the wolf is shut up'. Lady Goff suggests that she still resented the killing of Anne Askew, not by Gardiner but by others who shared his views.[11]

We saw how Katherine could be contemptuously dismissive of those who did not share her religious opinions, but there were still occasions when she helped or befriended some who disagreed with her. Her commitment to reform did not prevent her from appointing former conservative monks who had ties to her family to some of her livings, and she remained on good terms with some of her Lincolnshire neighbours who still adhered to the old faith. In Queen Elizabeth's reign she developed a cordial relationship with John Copledike, the son of a client of her late husband, who sent her gifts and occasionally visited her at Grimsthorpe, and was aided by Sir Edward Dymoke with whom she discussed a cousin's marriage prospects and shared remedies for rheumatism. Dymoke even agreed to use his influence to help secure a lucrative benefice for one of her 'godly' ministers, and offered to provide an alternative if he failed.[12] The inference is that her approach was essentially practical, and more tolerant than some of her statements would suggest.

Katherine could justifiably feel that the world was turning in her favour after many years of uncertainty, but all was not well in the Protestant camp. Protector Somerset was an able soldier who won a resounding victory over the Scots at Pinkie in September 1547, but his authoritarianism, his self-aggrandisement, coupled with his religious and social policies contrived to alienate almost all sections of society. A scheme to garrison the Lowlands in the aftermath of Pinkie failed to establish a permanent English presence in southern Scotland, and French backing for the Scots made it more difficult for the government to defend Boulogne and Calais. Landlords resented attempts to enforce the laws restricting enclosures (the seizing of common land for sheep grazing), but ordinary people in more religiously conservative areas of the country were no less offended by innovations that included the use of English in the first Book of Common Prayer (1549) and the whitewashing of church walls. A popular uprising against enclosures and in favour of 'the old and ancient religion' began in the West Country in May 1549 and spread quickly across southern England to East Anglia where a tanner and farmer named Robert Kett captured Norwich. Somerset vacillated between offering the rebels pardon and threatening them with the most dire consequences if they persisted in their opposition, and although the trouble was over by August it was thanks mainly to the determined action taken by John Dudley in Norfolk and Lord John Russell in the west. By now the great majority of the peers had lost confidence in the Protector's leadership, and he was committed to the Tower on 15 October. The conservatives, led by Wriothesley, would have had him charged with treason and executed, but the young king did not want to lose a second uncle and Dudley sought to win the boy's favour by arguing that his rival should be pardoned. The reprieve was only temporary, however. Attempts to recover his former authority brought him into renewed conflict with Dudley, and he was again arrested in October 1551, the same month that the latter was created Duke of Northumberland. This time there was no one to intercede for him, and he was executed on 22 January 1552.

Katherine would have found herself torn between her instincts as a landowner and her friend Hugh Latimer's sympathy for the peasants who protested against enclosures, but that was by no means her only difficulty. Early in 1550 she received a letter from William Cecil asking her to come to London to intercede with the Council on behalf of the imprisoned Somerset, but feared that her intervention at what was clearly a charged and delicate moment might only damage him:

The matter between the Council and my Lord and the state of his cause, seemeth by your letter not to differ from that which before I heard. But of my greater fear [presumably that Somerset would be executed] you have quieted me ... Wherefore I trust my journey will be less needful ... If I might be anyways persuaded that I might do my Lord any good I would gladly put myself in any venture for him. But alas, if I come and am not able to do for him that I would ... then shall I not only do him no good but rather harm ... I will bethink me how I can master that froward and crooked mind of mine before I come, and if I can bring that to pass then I will not fail with speed to accomplish your desire and mine.

Fortunately, just as she was penning her reply on 25 March she heard 'very good news and great hope' that the duke would soon be released and this decided her: 'Wherefore now, I am better determined to stay till their goodness be past, lest otherwise, if I come up whilst it is still moving, they think I come to take away their thanks.'[13]

Two months later Dudley proposed a marriage between

Katherine's eldest son Henry, now a youth of fifteen, and Anne Seymour, Somerset's daughter, but Katherine rejected it. Her reasons, set out in a letter to William Cecil, made much of her belief that the young couple should have some say in the matter, but she may have thought Somerset's recent troubles a bad omen and feared that his rehabilitation might only be temporary:

No unasked bonds between a boy and girl can give such assurance of good will as hath been tried already. And now they, marrying by our orders and without their consents, as they be yet without judgement to give such consent as ought to be given in matrimony, I cannot tell what more unkindness one of us might show another, or wherein we might work more wickedly than to bring our children into so miserable a state not to choose by their own liking … I know none this day living that I rather wish my son than she, but I am not, because I like her best, therefore desirous that she should be constrained by her friends to have him whom she might peradventure not like so well as I like her; neither can I yet assure myself of my son's liking … It is best that we keep our friendship and let our children follow our examples, to begin their loves of themselves without forcing them. Although both might feel bound by their parents' pleasures, the loss of their free choice is enough to break the greatest love.[14]

In the event Anne married Dudley's son Lord Lisle (the parties were presumably not prepared to wait to see if she and Henry developed an affection for one another), and Somerset was perhaps less than pleased with the whole business. Katherine wrote to Cecil in October complaining that he had paid scant regard to a suite of her cousin's, 'although', she added in a postscript, 'I could blame my lady [the Duchess of Somerset] for my lord's fault'.[15]

Young Henry Brandon had spent some time in the company of Edward VI, who was two years his junior, and early in 1549 visited France where he displayed his ability to ride wearing armour and made such a notable oration in Latin that those present 'wondered at his learning'.[16] He rejoined the king on his return, but that autumn Katherine decided that both her sons should complete their education at Cambridge University. Her choice of college was St John's, William Cecil's alma mater, and she rented a house in Kingston, a village five or six miles to the west of the city, in order to be near them. St John's had been founded by Henry VII's mother Margaret Beaufort, although the formal foundation charter was not sealed by her executors until 1511, two years after her death. Henry and Charles would have joined some 150 other undergraduates whose principal studies were in the fields of theology and the liberal arts.

We do not know how the boys responded to life at Cambridge, but they would have found the regime at the university very different to the comfortable existence they had enjoyed at Grimsthorpe or in London. They rose at between four and five in the morning, and spent an hour in prayer and listening to a sermon until six. They then attended lectures or studied with their tutors until ten when they paused for a frugal dinner of beef broth and oatmeal, after which they were subjected to another eleven or twelve hours of learning and 'reasoning' punctuated only by a supper 'not much better than the dinner' at around five. On retiring to their cold, unheated rooms at nine or ten at night, they would have shared the discomfort of other students who were obliged to 'walk or run up and down half an hour to get a heat on their feet' before going to bed.[17]

Even mealtimes afforded no opportunity for relaxation. The Cambridge don Thomas Wilson, who wrote a Latin life of the boys and who was to become a privy councillor in Queen Elizabeth's reign, observed how 'during dinner, one of them read a chapter of the Greek testament, and did afterwards translate into English; then they said Grace in turns; and did afterwards propound questions, either in philosophy or Divinity; and so spent all the time at meat in Latin disputation. When there was any public disputation, they were always present; every morning, they did read and afterwards translate some of Plato in Greek, and at supper present their labours. Every day was devoted to private lectures, and the residue they did account for'.[18] We can only hope that Henry and Charles enjoyed learning dead languages, and that there were occasions in their short lives when they were able to behave as boys usually do.

It was in Cambridge that Katherine formed a close but all too short-lived friendship with the German theologian Martin Bucer, who had come to England at the invitation of Archbishop Cranmer in April 1549 and had been appointed Regius Professor of Divinity before the end of the year. Bucer was almost thirty years older than Katherine and in poor health, but they spoke the same religious language. She is said to have attended some of his lectures, to have befriended his wife Wibrandis and their children when they arrived to join him, and to have helped to nurse him in the weeks before his death, probably from tuberculosis, in February 1551. Bucer's colleague Paul Fagius jokingly advised Wibrandis not to delay her coming to England 'because the Duchess of Suffolk is a widow'.[19]

Bucer's death must have caused Katherine great sadness, but worse was to follow. That summer there was an outbreak of the so-called 'sweating sickness' in Cambridge, and many left the city to avoid becoming infected. The sickness was a mystery illness which began with a sudden sense of apprehension, followed by sometimes violently cold shivers, giddiness, pain in the head, neck shoulders and limbs, and a general feeling of exhaustion. The 'cold' phase could last from half an hour to three hours, and was succeeded by the characteristic sweating accompanied by delirium, rapid pulse and intense thirst. Sufferers seldom recovered, and usually died within a day from a combination of lethargy and exhaustion. It was said to have been brought to England by the foreign mercenaries who landed at Milford Haven with Henry Tudor on 7 August 1485, although Thomas, Lord Stanley, had used it as an excuse to avoid joining Richard III about the 15th, a week before the battle was fought.[20]

Katherine's sons and their cousin George Stanley were sent first to Kingston, and then, after Stanley died, to Buckden, the home of Lady Margaret Neville, Catherine Parr's stepdaughter by her second marriage to Lord Latimer. But it was already too late. Thomas Wilson described their last hours as follows:

They both were together in one house, lodged in two separate chambers, and almost at one time both sickened, and both departed. They died both dukes, both well learned, both wise, and both right Godly. They both gave strange tokens of death to come. The elder, sitting at supper and very merry, said suddenly to that right honest matron and godly gentlewoman [probably Mrs Margaret Blakborn, who had acted as their governess and who would later share Katherine's exile], 'O Lord, where shall we sup tomorrow at night?' Whereupon, she being troubled, and yet saying comfortably, 'I trust, my Lord, either here, or elsewhere at some of your friends' houses.' 'Nay,' said he, 'we shall never sup together again in this world, be you well assured,' and with that, seeing the gentlewoman discomfited, turned it unto mirth, and passed the rest of his supper with much joy, and the same night after twelve of the clock, being the fourteenth of July, sickened, and so was taken the next morning, about seven of the clock, to the mercy of God. When the eldest was gone, the younger would not tarry, but told before (having no knowledge thereof by anybody living) of his brother's death, to the great wondering of all that were there, declaring what it was to lose so dear a friend, but comforting himself in that passion, said, 'Well, my brother is gone, but it makes no matter for I will go straight after him,' and so did within the space of half an hour.[21]

Elsewhere in his *Arte of Rhetorique*, Wilson is still more fulsome in his praise of the two youngsters:

Their towardness was such, and their gifts so great, that I know none which love learning, but hath sorrowed the lack of their being. And I know that the only [mere] naming of them will stir honest hearts to speak well of them ... In their youth, their father died, the eldest of them being not past nine years of age. After whose death their mother, knowing that wealth without wit is like a sword in a naked man's hand, and assuredly certain that knowledge would confirm judgement, provided so for their bringing up in all virtue and learning, that two like were not to be had within this realm again ... The elder's nature was such that he thought himself best when he was among the wisest, and yet contemned none, but thankfully used all, gentle in behaviour without childishness, stout of stomach without all pride, bold without all wariness and friendly with good advisement ... The other, keeping his book among the Cambridge men, profited (as they well know) both in virtue and learning, to their great admiration. For the Greek, the Latin, and the Italian, I know he could do more than would be thought true by my report. I leave to speak of his skill in pleasant instruments, neither will I utter his aptness in music, and his toward nature to all exercises of the body.[22]

Katherine was unwell at Kingston when her sons fell ill, and although she rose from her sickbed and hurried to Buckden when she received the news Henry died before she was able to reach him. She may have been able to comfort Charles in his last moments, and could have reflected on the cruel irony of how this disaster had come upon her in the very place her late husband had delivered his stark message to Catherine of Aragon eighteen years earlier. Her boys were buried in the church there with all the heraldic splendour to which they were entitled as, successively, the second and third dukes of Suffolk. Lady Goff speculates that an altar tomb now in the churchyard may be their memorial; if so it has presumably been moved from the interior of the building at some time in the intervening years.

The loss of both her children was a devastating blow, and Wilson wrote that 'I, seeing my Lady's Grace, their mother, taking their deaths most grievously, could not otherwise, for the duty which I then did, and ever shall owe unto her, but comfort her in that her heaviness, the which undoubtedly at that time, much weakened her body'.[23] He tried to console her by urging that

whereas for a time, your Grace much bewailed their lack, not only absenting yourself from all company, but also refusing all kind of comfort, almost dead with heaviness, your body being so worn with sorrow, that the long continuance of the same is much like to shorten your days: I will desire your Grace, for God's love, to refer your will to God's will, and whereas hitherto, nature has taught you to weep the lack of your natural children, let reason teach you hereafter to wipe away the tears ... How could your Grace think, that when you saw ancient wisdom in the one, and most pregnant wit in the other, marvellous sobriety in the elder and most laudable gentleness in the younger, both of them most studious in learning, most forward in all feats, as well of the body as of the mind, being two such and so excellent, that they were like long to continue with you ... And thus your Grace may ever rejoice, that you had two such, which lived so virtuously and died so Godly, and though their bodies be absent from your sight, yet the remembrance of their virtues shall never decay from your mind.[24]

Katherine doubtless appreciated his concern for her, but may have been less than impressed by his 'explanation' that God was punishing society for the policy of enclosure and the general wickedness of the era. Her sons had undoubtedly been saved from exposure to 'the danger of further evil and most vile wretchedness',[25] but she may have thought it a harsh punishment for her own sins and the sins of others.

The Spanish ambassador reported that the news of his young friends' deaths greatly saddened the boy king. Edward did not express his sorrow openly, but later devoted one of his orations to the subject of mourning the deaths of friends. Among other expressions of regret, the great Latinist Walter Haddon, another friend of Martin Bucer, delivered a eulogy, and Sir John Cheke, who was Regius Professor of Greek at Cambridge as well as the king's tutor, wrote an epitaph. Their appreciations, couched in similar terms to Wilson's, appear excessively laudatory to our way of thinking, but they were not alone. The Italian theologian

Peter Martyr, writing from Oxford to Henry Bullinger in Zurich on 6 August, expressed relief that he had not caught the 'English sweating sickness' himself, and remarked that

> what is grievously to be deplored [is that] we have lost some distinguished men; among whom was that most noble youth, the duke of Suffolk, the king's most intimate friend and contemporary, and brought up together with him. He was a youth of such hopes, that he was considered to have no equal for his age, the king's majesty alone excepted; and he had made such progress in learning, godliness, and piety, as to be the admiration of every one, and he would shortly have been a great support both to the state and the church. And, that nothing might be wanting to this calamity, his younger brother died with him: so that this summer has been by no means a happy one to the people of England.[26]

These men were all Protestants and accordingly well disposed towards Katherine, but there were others, adherents of the old religion, who saw the disaster differently. Wilson remarks that

> I know the wicked words of some ungodly folk have much disquieted your grace, notwithstanding, God being judge of your natural love towards your children, and all your faithful friends and servants, bearing earnest witness with your Grace of the same: their ungodly talk the more lightly it is to be esteemed, the more ungodly that it is. Nay, your Grace may rejoice rather, that whereas you have done well, you hear evil, according to the words of Christ. Blessed are you when men speak all evil things against you ... the harm is theirs which speak so lewdly, and the bliss theirs which bear it so patiently ... be your Grace therefore strong in adversity, and pray

for them that speak amiss of you, rendering good for evil, and with charitable dealing show yourself long suffering, so shall you heap coals on their heads.²⁷

It was easier for Katherine's religious opponents to argue that she was being punished because her faith was displeasing to God than it was for men like Wilson to portray the loss of her sons as somehow inevitable or as a kind of long-term benefit. But they had little hope of convincing her that they were right and she was wrong.

It is apparent that Katherine was now more than ever relying on William Cecil's wise counsel when she had a problem or felt uncertain, and that she set great store by the advice he gave her. Cecil had become Somerset's secretary in 1548, and had spent two months (November 1549–January 1550) in the Tower after the duke lost the protectorship. On his release he gravitated towards Dudley, becoming third secretary of state and a privy councillor, and his career did not suffer when Somerset was again arrested and executed. On the contrary, he was one of four men knighted when Dudley was created Duke of Northumberland, and he became increasingly prominent in the new government. He had proved himself a survivor, a man who could weather political storms and whose talents were valued by whoever might be in power.

Katherine would have been delighted to learn of her friend's promotions, partly on a personal level but also because his growing influence meant that he could intercede for her in her own causes. At various times in 1550 she sought his advice on how to approach the Council in her efforts to buy Spilsby chantry, and asked him to 'show his friendship to this poor bearer, in a certain suit that one of Jersey has against his brother … so that he may return to his garden, for until then I can have no salads or sweet herbs'. She also approached him about disputes which had arisen between her and the inhabitants of Spalding and Market Deeping (Lincs.) over a marsh and a common in her lordship of Pinchbeck and other rights, and sought on several occasions to defend her cousin William Naughton (or Nanton) against an excessive claim made against the proceeds of his office.[28] It was, perhaps, inevitable that she would unburden herself on her kind correspondent following her sons' deaths, and the letter she wrote to him in September 1551 suggests she had taken at least some of Wilson's admonitions to heart:

I give God thanks, good Master Cecil, for all His benefits, which it has pleased Him to heap upon me; and truly I take this last (and to the first sight, most sharp and bitter) punishment not for the least of His benefits; inasmuch as I have never been so well taught by any other before to know His power, His love and mercy, my own weakness and that wretched state that without Him I should endure here. And to ascertain you that I have received great comfort in Him, I would gladly do it by talk and sight of you. But as I confess myself no better than flesh, so I am not well able with quiet to behold my very friends without some parts of these vile dregs of Adam to seem sorry for that whereof I know I ought rather to rejoice …[29]

There can be no doubt that the whole episode drained Katherine both physically and emotionally, and she was to lose more than her sons and her tranquillity. Tattershall and other properties granted to her husband and his male issue automatically reverted to the Crown, and on 4 October, the day Dudley became Duke of Northumberland and Cecil was knighted, King Edward created

Henry Grey, Marquis of Dorset, her stepdaughter Frances's husband, Duke of Suffolk. Katherine did not resent this – on the contrary, she spent Christmas with Henry and Frances and their daughters Jane (the future 'nine days' queen'), Catherine and Mary – and seems to have regained much of her old composure. Hugh Latimer again became a regular guest at Grimsthorpe, and in June 1552 Katherine sent William Cecil a buck which she had helped to catch herself. Her accompanying letter included an invitation to hunt in her park when it pleased him 'for I am very glad when any of my friends may have their pastime here, and nothing grieves me more but when I cannot make their pastime with them', and there is more than a hint of a renewed zest for life in her closing salutation: 'And so, with my hearty commendations ... from Grimsthorpe this present Wednesday at six o'clock in the morning and like a sluggard in my bed [!].'[30]

Katherine was presumably an early riser in normal circumstances, but a postscript she added to her letter gives a clue to her newfound enthusiasm: 'Master Bertie is at London to conclude if he can with the heirs. For I would gladly discharge the trust wherein my Lord [her late husband] did leave me before I did for any man's pleasure anything else.'[31] 'Master Bertie' as we have already noted, was Richard Bertie, Katherine's gentleman-usher, a trusted official whose ceremonial role was to walk ahead of her in procession but who also transacted a good deal of business for her. Two years older than his mistress, he had received a Bachelor of Arts degree from Corpus Christi College, Oxford, in 1537, and then spent a short time in the household of Lord Chancellor Wriothesley. He spoke French, Italian and Latin fluently, and – what may have been his greatest recommendation in Katherine's eyes – he was steadfastly Protestant. Her desire to settle her late husband's affairs before she 'did for any man's pleasure anything else' could imply that she was considering remarriage, and that she had already formed an attachment to the man who now shouldered much of the burden of running Grimsthorpe and who had safeguarded her interests during her time of trouble. There were, very possibly, those who tut-tutted that the dowager Duchess of Suffolk was marrying beneath herself, but Katherine would have weighed her options carefully. She would have to defer to her husband as the new master of her properties and household, but wedding a commoner ensured that she retained her social seniority and with it a measure of independence.[32] She and Richard Bertie were married, very probably by Hugh Latimer, either in July 1552 or at the beginning of 1553.

It is somewhat remarkable that Bertie had reached the then very mature age of thirty-six without (so far as we know) having been married previously. It is possible to suggest that he had been waiting for the right opportunity, that he had always hoped to find a wife whose wealth and social standing would enhance his own prospects; but events would prove that he was genuinely devoted to Katherine and not without reason. Like Thomas Wilson, he presumably admired her because she was 'of birth noble, and wit [intelligence] great, of nature gentle, and merciful to the poor, and to the godly, and especially to the learned an earnest good patroness and most helping lady above all other',[33] but we have already seen that she could also be acerbic and difficult to live with. She was indisputably a good 'catch', but there would certainly have been occasions when Bertie had to watch his step.

It will already be apparent that a good deal of what we know of Katherine's own thoughts and feelings is derived from her personal letters, and from her ability to write them herself.[34] Today, we assume that reading and writing are mutually complementary, but, as Alison Sim points out, one is considerably more difficult than the other and it is possible to be able to read but not to write.[35] Over a hundred letters composed by Margaret Paston, the matriarch of the famous Norfolk gentry family, survive from the latter half of the fifteenth century, although it is clear from internal evidence that she could not write herself. Rather, her correspondence tends to be in the same hand within certain time periods, indicating that she used the services of whichever clerk or literate member of the family happened to be available. But this is not to say that she was unable to read the replies.

One aspect of Katherine's life that becomes evident from her regular correspondence with William Cecil is how frequently she travelled and changed her abode. In one period of nine months, from May 1550 to February 1551, she was at Kingston in May, at Eresby in August, at Stamford on 3 September, back at Eresby five days later, at Grimsthorpe on the 18th of the month, at Tattershall on 1 October, at Stamford again on 15 November, and in Cambridge the following February before returning to Grimsthorpe. There must have been other travels and sojourns when no letter was sent to Cecil, and the question is whether they were all strictly necessary or whether they reflect a particular trait in her character. As we have seen, she went to Kingston and Cambridge to visit her sons, but it is unclear if the other moves were brief and personal or involved relocating a significant part of the household. Some may have been necessitated by the need to periodically 'sweeten' Grimsthorpe, but there is no hint that she disliked these upheavals or sought to avoid them. We do not know how she preferred to travel, but at this time of her life she almost certainly preferred horseback, perhaps side-saddle, to the bumpy alternative of a carriage.

Katherine may have felt that the past few years had already dispensed more than their fair share of tragedy, but fate had not finished with her yet. The youthful King Edward was displaying great promise and many thought he would prove as magnificent a ruler as his late father. In 1551 the Venetian ambassador Daniel Barbaro described him as handsome, affable and of 'becoming stature', and noted that in physical activity, literary study and linguistic ability he 'appears to surpass his comrades and competitors'. He practised the use of arms every day on horseback, hunted regularly, and delighted 'in every sort of exercise, drawing the bow, playing rackets, hunting and so forth, indefatigably'. It was with his approval that the 1552 Book of Common Prayer abolished old ceremonies that had hitherto been retained along with prayers for the dead together with all references to the Virgin, saints and prophets, and that the forty-two articles of faith published a year later affirmed the Protestant doctrine of justification by faith alone, declared transubstantiation 'repugnant to the plain words of scripture' and condemned the ceremonies of the Mass as 'fables and dangerous deceits'. Protestants like Katherine looked forward to a reign in which their religion would be promoted by a king who was fiercely committed to it, but their hopes were about to be shattered. Edward had contracted what he described in his journal as 'the measles and the smallpox' in April 1552, and although he appeared to recover quickly the illness left behind it a fatal legacy. Modern research has shown that measles can suppress natural immunity to tuberculosis, reactivating the bacteria that can survive within healthy lung tissue, and it was to tuberculosis that he succumbed after a period of increasing debility on 6 July 1553. Some further change was now inevitable, but few could have anticipated how dramatic it would prove to be.[36]

5

THE BID FOR THE THRONE
1553–1554*

When Henry VIII made his last will in December 1546 he bequeathed his throne to his son Edward (as he was bound to do), but some of his other instructions raised eyebrows. If Edward died childless the throne was to pass to his half-sister Mary (notwithstanding that she had been declared illegitimate and there was no precedent for a queen regnant), and if she failed to produce a child it would pass to the no less 'illegitimate' Elizabeth. The next heirs were to be the descendants of Henry's younger sister Mary – the male offspring of Katherine Willoughby's stepdaughters Frances Grey and Eleanor Clifford – but there was no place for the line of his elder sister Margaret, represented by Mary, Queen of Scots. No previous king had tried to determine the succession in this manner, but Henry was a law unto himself.

There were, of course, sound practical reasons why a woman could not rule a country as well as the more misogynistic arguments of zealots like Knox and Becon. Women could not, did not, lead armies into battle (no one would have cited Joan of Arc as an 'example' of a female who had done precisely that), and there was also the vexed question of the queen's marriage. The husband of a reigning queen would expect to become king consort and govern with and for her – a situation which could exacerbate internal rivalries if she wed one of her own subjects or could threaten national interests if she chose a foreigner. A 'king' from a friendly Protestant country could be tolerated, but what if the queen took a husband from France or, still worse, Spain?

These thoughts weighed heavily on the mind of the Duke of Northumberland when it became apparent that Edward VI was dying. If the Catholic Princess Mary succeeded she would almost certainly seek to restore the old religion, and there was no guarantee that he and his family would retain their pre-eminence in government even if the Crown passed to the Protestant Princess Elizabeth. Frances and the now deceased Eleanor were the mothers of daughters, but Frances had not had a child for eight years and the daughters were all unmarried. Northumberland could have pressed Edward to restore Frances to her natural place in the succession, but he did not do so – perhaps because few relished the prospect of her ineffectual husband Henry Grey becoming king consort. Instead, he focused his attention on Lady Jane, Frances's eldest surviving child, whose accession, it seemed to him, would secure the future of both Protestantism and his own house.

So much has been written about Lady Jane Grey that it would be superfluous to chart her young life in any detail. Suffice it to say that she was as committed to Protestantism as her step-grandmother and precocious to a fault. Born, probably, in May 1537 (six months before Edward VI),[1] she was sent at the tender age of ten to live with Queen Catherine Parr and her new husband Thomas Seymour. It was Seymour (whose mad schemes to wed Princess Elizabeth and capture the young king have already been noticed) who had convinced her parents that he could 'arrange' her marriage to Edward, and who persuaded them to allow her to rejoin his household after she had returned home following Catherine Parr's death. But his ambitions were greater than his influence, and nothing had been accomplished when he was executed for treason. Fate had freed Jane from the clutches of one political manipulator, but was about to deliver her into the hands of another.

It is unclear when Northumberland first contemplated solving the 'problem' of the succession by making Jane queen, but the plan was certainly forming in his mind when he accepted a suggestion (made, possibly, by the resolutely Protestant Marquis of Northampton) that she should marry his fifth and youngest son Guildford in April 1553.[2] At the same time her sister Catherine would wed Lord Herbert, the son of his ally the Earl of Pembroke, and his own daughter (also Catherine) would be joined to the eldest son of another potential supporter, the Earl of Huntingdon. The three couples were united in marriage at Durham House, the duke's London home, on 25 May, but in circumstances that reflected the contrived nature of the occasion. The king was too ill to be present, the two princesses were not invited, and the two Grey girls seem to have returned home with their parents after the ceremony.[3] The reasons for this are uncertain because Jane, now just sixteen, was old enough to live with her husband even if the same could not be said of the twelve-year-old Catherine. It has been suggested that Northumberland thought that non-consummation would make the annulment of their unions easier if the political situation changed (if, by some chance, his scheme faltered),[4] but it was perhaps at the insistence of Jane's father, who realised that his own family would lose its pre-eminence if she gave birth to a Dudley son.

If Katherine Willoughby was among the 'great concourse of the principal persons of the kingdom'[5] who attended this grand wedding she would have seen the three young couples attired in silver and gold fabrics (valuables seized from the executed Duke of Somerset) obediently complying with their parents' wishes. Undoubtedly, she would have disapproved of the overtly political nature of the unions, a criticism justified by Jane and Guildford's apparent want of affection for one another and by the lack of concern for Pembroke's son Lord Herbert, who had been brought from his sickbed to stand beside Catherine. If she saw the king or heard rumours about his health during her visit she may have begun to suspect where events were leading and discussed the situation with Frances or William Cecil, but she would not have supposed that this would be the last time she would see the Duke of Northumberland and some of his – and her – other friends.

Soon after the onset of what was to be Edward's last illness, he decided to put his own plans for the succession into writing. Only a few strokes of the pen were needed to exclude Frances and her daughters, the Scottish line, and his two half-sisters,[6] but the problem was that none of his preferred male successors – Frances's son(s) and grandson(s) – had yet been born. There was every reason, at that point, to assume that such an heir would soon be forthcoming, but as Edward's health deteriorated he was obliged to accept that the next sovereign would be a woman. He could have nominated Frances as a short-term 'caretaker', but decided – or was persuaded – that her eldest daughter would prove a better guarantor of his religious settlement. Northumberland must have watched with great satisfaction as Edward returned to his 'device for the succession' and bequeathed his crown to '*the Lady Jane and her heirs male*' (my italics).

Francis and her husband must have been disappointed that her prior claim had again been passed over, and if they expressed disquiet they were not alone. Archbishop Cranmer and others argued that Henry VIII's arrangements, which had been ratified by Act of Parliament, could only be changed by the passing of another Act; and it was with great reluctance that the law officers compiled a formal document from the king's scrawled handwriting. Between 21 June and 8 July no fewer than 202 notables – including Cranmer and some bishops, twenty-four peers, the judges and the mayor of London – signed this 'declaration' and swore a solemn oath to uphold its provisions. They were promised pardon if they were subsequently accused of committing a capital offence by acceding to Edward's wishes (the Treasons Act of 1547 had made it illegal to change his father's settlement), but it is unlikely that many were reassured.

Edward and Northumberland's problem was that a king's authority died with him. He could not compel his successor to pursue a particular policy, nor bind those who would rule during a minority. Henry VIII had recognised this when he had his plans for the succession enshrined in an Act of Parliament, but such an Act – and even the Act that made it a capital offence to change it – could be repealed if a later Parliament thought it necessary. The obvious course of action was to summon a new Parliament for this purpose, but it was becoming increasingly apparent that Edward would not live to see its business concluded. The result was that whatever the young king said or did in the meantime, his father's wishes remained the law of the land.

It may be worth pausing for a moment here to consider

the rights and wrongs of all this. Was Jane the rightful heir at common law and Mary a bastard, or was Mary her father's chosen successor and Jane an interloper? At the heart of the matter was the question of whether Henry VIII and his first 'wife' Catherine of Aragon had been legally married. If they had, then Mary was legitimate and her half-brother Edward's lawful successor: but if not then she was illegitimate and no more entitled to her father's property than any other bastard. Although Henry had nominated her to succeed if Edward died without issue he had done nothing to change her illegitimate status; and the idea that a king could choose his successor (any successor) in what he perceived to be the national interest was without precedent. No Act of Parliament could deprive a rightful sovereign of his or her inheritance, and Jane (or, more specifically, Frances), had an entirely valid claim.

It would not, however, be easy to dispossess Mary, who enjoyed widespread popularity and who had been regarded as heir apparent for much of the past decade. One course of action would have been for Northumberland and his associates to circulate Edward's 'Declaration' throughout the country, but they realised that to do so would risk triggering a pro-Marian reaction. In the last weeks of Edward's life Mary moved from Newhall in Sussex to Hunsdon in Hertfordshire in anticipation of a summons to the capital, but at some point she was warned of what was afoot in London and retired to the relative safety of Kenninghall in Norfolk. Robert Dudley and 300 horsemen were sent to Hunsdon to arrest her the day after Edward's death on 6 July (perhaps the earliest that his father dared move against her openly), but by then it was already too late.

Northumberland did not immediately announce that Edward had died, but a rumour reached Jehan Scheyfve, the Imperial ambassador, on 7 July, and was soon common knowledge in London. Both Scheyfve and the French ambassador Antoine de Noailles thought the duke's power was unchallengeable, but Mary had no intention of surrendering what she believed was her divinely ordained right to succeed her brother. Two days later, on the 9th, Jane was brought to Syon House in Isleworth (another of Northumberland's London properties), knowing nothing of the king's death or what it would mean for her. On being informed that she was to supplant Mary she collapsed, weeping, and startled those present by protesting that the Crown was not her right. Northumberland and her parents met her defiance by angrily insisting that it was her duty to obey them, and, isolated and uncertain, she bowed to their wishes. Next day she was escorted to the Tower with Guildford (with whom she was now living), and there 'received as queen'.

There is no evidence that Katherine Willoughby personally witnessed this momentous occasion, and it is possible to imagine her at home at Grimsthorpe in the early stages of pregnancy anxiously awaiting news of every development. Frances was her stepdaughter, Jane her step-granddaughter, and Northumberland an old friend; but so too was Princess Mary, who had played cards with her in the days when they both favoured the old religion. Her first response would have been to write to William Cecil seeking his assessment of the situation, but the prudent Cecil would surely have destroyed any letter that appeared to endorse Jane's accession. It can only be assumed that, privately at least, she gave the conspirators her blessing, but perhaps not without some feelings of sympathy for Mary, whose mother had been so close to hers.

In the Tower Jane was treated with all the deference and respect due to a queen awaiting her coronation, but continued to question the wisdom of her decision. She declined to try on the crown to see if it fitted her, and precipitated the first clash of her 'reign' by refusing her husband the title of king. She met his reproaches and the anger of his mother, the Duchess of Northumberland, with the firm statement that she would do nothing unconstitutional (i.e. without the consent of Parliament), and found – for the first time – that her orders were obeyed. The lords of the Council must have been dismayed by her defiance and by the realisation that this slip of a girl who they had placed over them was minded to be her own person; but they could not refuse her without compromising their claim to be her loyal subjects. Still more alarming was that on 10 July a letter was received from Mary declaring her assumption that she had succeeded her brother, and promising pardon all who would submit to her. Any lingering hopes that she would simply accept the situation or perhaps retire into exile effectively vanished, and to make matters worse, it was becoming clear that there was little or no popular enthusiasm for Jane's accession. Bishop Ridley had tried to rally support for her in a sermon preached at St Paul's on the Sunday, but had been met by what one writer describes as 'a mixture of grief and rage'.[7]

From 10 to 13 July the Council met in the Tower while Guildford, the would-be 'king', dined in regal isolation and, according to one source, chaired its deliberations.[8] Jane did not attend personally, and was probably unaware of the tensions that now existed between Northumberland and some of the other nobles. It was decided the Duke of Suffolk would lead an army into East Anglia to apprehend Mary while Northumberland maintained the government in the capital; but Jane insisted that her father, who was unwell, should remain with her and so Northumberland (reluctantly, perhaps because he did not altogether trust his colleagues), undertook to lead it himself. His force left the capital on either Thursday 13 or Friday 14 July, and marched some twenty-five miles to Ware (Herts.).

Northumberland's decision to obey Jane and go in pursuit of Mary was a fundamental error. He was a more experienced soldier than Suffolk, but the situation did not call for great leadership. What it did require was the personal intervention of a nobleman who was well known in the region and whose popularity there could rival Mary's – qualities that Suffolk possessed in some measure but Northumberland did not. It is also apparent that his absence loosened his grip on the situation by making it virtually impossible for him to dominate the Council from a distance. Councillors who would not have opposed him to his face began to weigh their options and consider how they might exculpate themselves in the event of a Marian victory. They had promised to support Jane and would, presumably, have preferred her to reign over them, but it was prudent to have a foot in both camps.

Northumberland proceeded cautiously, gathering more troops as he went – his sons joined him at Ware on Friday – and reached Cambridge on 15 July. He lingered there for three days, probably to allow time for his artillery and supply train to catch up with his cavalry, before advancing to Bury St Edmunds on Tuesday 18th. Mary had been assembling forces at her new, more secure, base at Framlingham, and little more than a day's march now separated the two armies; but instead of launching the decisive attack everyone expected Northumberland returned to Cambridge. In all probability, he had learned that Mary's force was much larger and better equipped than he had anticipated,[9] and his situation became hopeless when he was informed, probably in the early hours of the

20th, that many of the colleagues he had left behind in London had changed sides. That afternoon he proclaimed Mary in Cambridge marketplace, and dismissed his now demoralised troops.

It is unclear if the councillors in London were swayed mainly by their dislike of Northumberland's bullying attitude or by their awareness of the groundswell of support for Mary, but they were anxious to exonerate themselves while they still had the opportunity. Their options were limited while they were effectively confined to the Tower, so they told Jane that their best course of action was to ask the French ambassador to help them hire mercenaries. The French, they argued, feared that Mary would ally England to her cousin the Emperor if she gained the ascendancy; but no sooner had they regained their freedom than they assembled at Baynard's Castle, the Earl of Pembroke's London residence, and denounced Jane as a usurper. They declared Northumberland a traitor and wrote to him, ordering him to surrender and dismiss his army; and as Mary was proclaimed in the capital to scenes of rejoicing, two of their number returned to the Tower to tell Suffolk that his daughter's reign was over. Suffolk tore the canopy from above Jane's chair and told her that she must now be content with a private life, to which she retorted that she had never desired any other and willingly relinquished the Crown. He then sought to save his own skin by proclaiming Mary on Tower Hill before making his way to Sheen Palace, leaving Jane and Guildford bewildered and alone.

Soon after Northumberland had proclaimed Mary in Cambridge the university sergeant-at-arms and others tried to arrest him, but he managed to overawe his would-be captors and retain his liberty for a few more hours. He spent most of this time orchestrating an escape plan with his sons and a few committed supporters, but they were arrested by some members of the royal guard who had marched with them even before the Earl of Arundel arrived to take them into official custody. The prisoners left Cambridge on 24 July, and next day, when they arrived in London, Northumberland was obliged to ride through a mob whose anger could scarcely be restrained by his armed escort. It is said that he never flinched or trembled beneath the hail of filth, stones and insults, but that Warwick, his eldest son, was overcome, covered his face, and burst into tears.

During the eleven days that separated Northumberland's capture from Mary's entry into London, Jane and her remaining four servants were removed from the Tower proper to the Gentleman-Gaoler's lodgings on Tower Green. Guildford was imprisoned in the Beauchamp Tower where he was soon joined by his father and brothers together with the Marquis of Northampton, their acolytes Sir John Gates and Sir Thomas Palmer, and others. Mary tacitly forgave those members of the Council who, less than a fortnight previously, had declared her a bastard and a rebel, and rejected the entreaties of Scheyfve's successor Simon Renard that Jane should be executed to prevent further trouble. She formally pardoned Suffolk on 30 July after granting Frances a private audience, and made it clear that she had no desire to instigate a political or religious bloodbath. In her pronouncement of 18 August she stated that although she 'would be glad' if her people were reconciled to Catholicism she was 'minded not to compel' them, and begged them not to use 'those new-found devilish terms of papist or heretic'. This contrasts strikingly with a letter Jane wrote a few weeks later in which she described Catholics as Romish anti-Christians, their church as the 'Whore of Babylon' and urged her correspondent to turn from 'the most wicked Mass'.[10]

Northumberland, Warwick and Northampton were brought to trial at Westminster Hall on 18 August, to be followed by Gates, Palmer, Palmer's brother Henry, and Northumberland's brother Sir Andrew Dudley the next day. Lady Jane, Guildford, and the others were to be dealt with later. The examinations were formal and the verdicts predetermined – it had already been decided that only Northumberland, Gates and Palmer would die – although Northumberland still hoped for clemency. He argued that he had acted only by warrant of the Great Seal of England and with the approval of the other members of the Council who were therefore, *ipso facto*, equally guilty; but the president, the Duke of Norfolk, replied that the seal had no valid authority in the hands of a usurper, and until such lords as might be accused were formally convicted their right to judge him could not be questioned! Sentence being passed, he asked for the favour of beheading (quicker and more dignified that being hanged, drawn and quartered), and for time to be reconciled to the Catholic faith. This was perhaps, his last desperate bid for pardon, but it bought him only one extra day of life. Jane, seeing her father-in-law pass by on his way to Mass in the Tower chapel, dismissed his change of heart as false and evil. 'I pray God,' she remarked afterwards, '[that] I, nor no friend of mine, die so.'[11]

Northumberland was executed on 22 August, and Jane embarked on the last six months of her life as the Gentleman-Gaoler's prisoner. Her movements were inevitably restricted, but she retained the services of her four servants, had an ample allowance for her upkeep, and could dine with the gaoler when she chose. On 14 November she was taken to the Guildhall where she was tried together with Guildford and Ambrose and Henry Dudley (Northumberland's second and third sons), and

Archbishop Cranmer. All the accused pleaded guilty and were formally sentenced to death, but none now expected to be executed. A period of imprisonment was inevitable, but the clemency that had allowed the crimes of others to go unpunished would surely be extended to them.

It is likely that all those involved in the conspiracy would have been pardoned (eventually) if the situation had remained calm and unthreatening, but they had not reckoned with the backlash provoked by Mary's wish to marry Philip of Spain. Only three days after the trial the Council begged her, in the strongest terms, to wed an Englishman, but she replied that marriage to a husband she did not care for 'would be her death'.[12] The old enmity against the Spanish manifested itself in a wave of crudely expressed insularity, and soon there were whisperings that Jane or Elizabeth would be used as the figurehead of a rebellion designed not to depose Mary but to force her to change her plans. Mary displayed her mistrust by requiring the lords to sign a paper in which each formally approved of the match; but in January 1554 Suffolk (who had not signed) came out in rebellion with Sir Thomas Wyatt (a Kentish Catholic who had declared for Mary the previous summer), and Sir Peter Carew in the west. It must have seemed that nearly everyone – Catholic and Protestant alike – supported the enterprise, and there was really no prospect of failure; but Suffolk's attempt to raise the Midlands faltered when the Earl of Huntingdon (on whom he was relying for support) held Coventry against him, and Wyatt's march on London was defeated by the Earl of Pembroke at Charing Cross. Suffolk was captured at his manor of Astley (Warks.), hiding in the hollow trunk of a tree as the story has it, and joined his daughter in the Tower a few days later. Jane had played no part in the uprising, but her claim to the throne, her wearing of the crown the previous summer, had brought the danger she still posed into sharp focus. Mary had been shaken by the experience, and a satisfied Renard sat down to inform the Emperor that 'at last Jane of Suffolk and her husband are to lose their heads'.[13]

It would be easy to suppose that these two rival queens, both members of the extended Tudor royal family, felt only bitterness towards one another: but Mary displayed commendable concern for her young second cousin's spiritual welfare by sending her personal chaplain, John Feckenham, to visit Jane in prison. Feckenham was kind, clever and tolerant, and was sufficiently encouraged by their first meeting to ask Mary to postpone the sentence for a few days so that he could discuss Jane's religious opinions with her. He was later credited with converting John Cheke, Edward VI's tutor, to Catholicism, but if he hoped to convince Jane of the error of her beliefs he was to be disappointed. 'As for my heavy case, I thank God I do so little lament it ... being a thing so profitable for my soul's health,' she told him, and the best he could do was to persuade her to dispute the differences between them, a debate which culminated in a long and fruitless discussion of the doctrine of transubstantiation. At last Feckenham had to acknowledge that he was beaten. 'I am sorry for you,' he said as they parted, 'for I am sure that we two shall never meet (i.e. in heaven).' 'True it is,' Jane is said to have replied, 'that we shall never meet except God turn your heart';[14] but she agreed to allow him to accompany her to the scaffold when the time came. Jane was probably not a little disturbed by these encounters, perhaps not so much by Feckenham's arguments as by his undeniable goodness. As a Catholic he represented the forces of evil; but he was gentle, wise and virtuous, quite unlike the devious, self-seeking

Protestants who had used and then abandoned her when their schemes faltered. If he was good there must, logically, be other Catholics who were honourable even if they were mistaken, and she began to realise that not everything was quite as black or white as she had once thought.

In spite of their differences Feckenham was sufficiently impressed by Jane to again ask the queen to show mercy, but his efforts were thwarted by Bishop Gardiner, who had been released from prison when Mary entered London and who was now her Lord Chancellor. On Sunday 11 February Gardiner preached a powerful sermon before Mary in her private chapel in which he equated Protestantism with treason and emphasised how some of those she had pardoned for their part in the July conspiracy had been responsible for the more recent troubles. He was a formidable figure, with 'frowning brows, eyes an inch within the head ... [and] great paws like the devil' according to John Ponet, the Protestant Edwardian Bishop of Winchester,[15] and he exhorted Mary to be 'merciful to the body of the commonwealth' rather than to undeserving individuals who deserved only to be 'cut off and consumed'.[16] He had no reason to love any member of the House of Suffolk, but we can only wonder how far Katherine Willoughby's studied rudeness towards him had hardened his attitude towards Jane.

The execution of Jane and Guildford the following day must have appalled Katherine, but being on the point of giving, or having just given, birth to Suzan, her first child by Richard Bertie, she could do nothing to prevent it. If she wrote to Queen Mary begging clemency for the young couple her letter has not survived, and she may have feared that, as with Somerset years earlier, her intervention would do more harm than good. She could have held

Northumberland and Suffolk primarily responsible for what had happened, but one was her friend and the other her stepdaughter's husband. From a Protestant perspective they had given their lives to preserve true religion and prevent Mary's Spanish marriage (Suffolk had gone to the block ten days after Jane), and she surely regarded them as patriots and martyrs. It is more likely that, in her eyes, the real culprits were the nobles who had sworn to maintain Jane as queen but who had betrayed both her and their faith at the first opportunity, men for whom she now felt nothing but contempt. A dark cloud had descended on both Grimsthorpe and Protestant England, and she could only wonder how her family and her religion would fare now.

6

ESCAPE
1554–1555

It will be evident from the little that has been written this far that Lady Jane's supporters can be divided into two distinct groups: those who were forgiven by Queen Mary (even if, in many cases, they had to pay dearly for the privilege), and those who were not. Katherine's two closest friends, Hugh Latimer and William Cecil, fared very differently. Of the two, Cecil's involvement was undoubtedly the greater, but he was a layman and a politician. Latimer was both more committed and less slippery, and in Mary's eyes an incorrigible heretic. The fate of the former would have given Katherine grounds for optimism, but the latter's would have brought her close to despair.

William Cecil now held the position of third secretary, and as a member of the Council had signed Edward's 'Declaration' and fulfilled his duties during Jane's short 'reign'. He submitted to Mary at the first opportunity, claiming that he had signed the document with great reluctance and that he had attended Council meetings only when 'sent for', i.e. when he had no alternative.[1] The truth of this cannot now be established, neither can his other assertions that he had secretly blocked orders to supply men and horses to Northumberland's army, plotted with the Marquis of Winchester to gain control of Windsor Castle (for Mary), and personally won over the Earl of Arundel and Lord Darcy. Mary forgave him, partly perhaps because his sister-in-law, Anne Bacon, was one of her favourites; and although he retired from public office he remained on good terms with her government during the difficult next five years.

Hugh Latimer was less fortunate. Appointed Bishop of Worcester in 1535, he had been obliged to resign his see when he opposed Henry VIII's stance on some traditional theological doctrines four years later. He resumed his advocacy of reform under Edward, but his forthright condemnation of Catholic beliefs was anathema to his opponents in Mary's party. He could not, would not, seek to excuse himself after the manner of a Cecil, and made no attempt to slip quietly into exile after Jane's 'reign' ended. For a time he lived at his family home at Baxterley (Warks.), but was arrested in September 1553 and burned at the stake with Bishop Ridley two years later. Katherine paid for the publication of many of his sermons from 1548 onwards, and it is thanks to her (and to his amanuensis, his Swiss servant Augustine Bernher), that so many of his words can be read today.[2]

Katherine's political and religious opinions were as well documented as Cecil's and Latimer's, but she presented an altogether more difficult target than a county knight and an ex-bishop. Lord Chancellor Gardiner seems to have accepted that her recent confinement made it impractical to summon her to London (or perhaps he did not relish a face-to-face confrontation with this feistiest of opponents), and it was Richard Bertie he ordered to appear before him. He could have requested Bertie's

1. Katherine Willoughby, Duchess of Suffolk, in a detail of a portrait painted in 1548 when she was twenty-nine. Her first husband, Charles Brandon, had died three years earlier, and she married Richard Bertie, her gentleman-usher, in 1552 or 1553.

2. Charles Brandon, Duke of Suffolk, portrayed in his later years when he was married to Katherine. An engraving by W. H. Mote published in *Portraits and Memoirs of the Most Illustrious Personages of British History Encyclopedia* in 1836.

3. Westhorpe (Suffolk). The three-arched Tudor bridge over the moat. Katherine lived in the now demolished brick and figurative terracotta mansion as the ward of Charles Brandon, Duke of Suffolk, who she married after his third wife, Mary Tudor, died in 1533.

4. Westhorpe (Suffolk). Charles Brandon's arms, now set into the outer wall of Westhorpe Hall Residential Care Home.

5 & 6. Westhorpe (Suffolk). Some of the heraldic images that once adorned the hall were recovered when the moat was cleared in the 1990s. The heraldry displayed included Charles Brandon's crowned lion with a protruding tongue and the Tudor rose.

Left: 7. Mary Tudor, Katherine's surrogate mother between 1528 and 1533, a portrait in St Mary's church, Bury St Edmunds. The original was painted *c.* 1514 by Jean Perréal, Royal Painter at the French Court, for her first husband, King Louis XII, shortly before she left England for France.

Below: 8. Mary Tudor's grave in St Mary's church, Bury St Edmunds. Her remains were brought here at the dissolution of the nearby abbey.

MARY TUDOR
1495-1533
Queen of France

Sacred to the Memory of MARY TUDOR, Third Dau.r of HENRY ye 7: KING of ENGLAND, and QUEEN of FRANCE; Who was first married in 1514, to LEWIS ye 12:th KING of FRANCE, and afterwards in 1517, to CHARLES BRANDON DUKE of SUFFOLK. She died in His Life Time in 1533, at ye Manor of WESTHORP in this Coun.y and was interr'd in ye same Year in ye Monastery of St EDMUND'S BURY, and was removed into this Church, after ye Dissolution of the Abbey.

Right: 9. Stained-glass window by Clayton and Bell in St Mary's church, Bury St Edmunds, depicting events in Mary Tudor's life. The scenes portrayed are:
Upper lights, from left to right: Mary's marriage to Louis XII at Abbeville; her entry into Paris; mourning her late husband at Cluny; Erasmus and Sir Thomas More visit the royal children at Eltham; Mary's abortive betrothal to Charles of Ghent (afterwards Charles V), at Richmond in 1508; her departure from Dover in October 1514.
Lower lights: Mary's marriage to Charles Brandon in the chapel at Cluny; their reconciliation with Henry VIII at their second marriage at Greenwich; Mary's funeral in St Edmund's abbey.

Below: 10. Bradgate House in Bradgate Park, Leicestershire, home of Charles and Mary Brandon's daughter Frances and her family. Katherine would have been a regular visitor here in the 1530s and 1540s.

11. Catherine of Aragon, Henry VIII's first wife. A statue by Manuel Gonzalez Muñoz erected in 2007 at the Archbishop's Palace in Alcalá de Henares, where she was born.

12. Anne Boleyn, a pen-and-ink sketch by Holbein. Katherine and her mother had little time for a woman who, for them, was never more than the king's mistress.

Above: 13. A young Princess
Mary, *c.* 1536. She played
cards and corresponded with
Katherine when they were
both Roman Catholics, but
their relationship deteriorated
badly after Katherine became
a Protestant.

Right: 14. Jane Seymour,
Henry VIII's third wife, and
the only one to give him a
son. He amused himself with
Katherine after her death in
1537.

Left: 15. Tattershall Castle, Lincolnshire, the great tower from the east. Built by Ralph, Lord Cromwell between 1430 and 1450, it was one of Katherine's principal residences between 1537 and 1551. Only the timely intervention of Lord Curzon saved it from demolition in 1911.

Below: 16. Tattershall Castle. The ornately decorated fifteenth-century fireplace in the Great Hall, one of four in the building. The heraldry includes the arms of families associated with the Cromwells together with St George slaying the dragon and two Treasurer's purses. (Lord Cromwell was Henry VI's Treasurer.)

17. Tattershall Castle. The beautifully carved sixteenth-century chest in the Audience Chamber. The furniture now in the castle was purchased by Lord Curzon in the early years of the twentieth century, so it is not thought that the carvings represent Katherine, Richard Bertie and their two children.

18. Tattershall Castle. The view from the battlements looking east. The scene is dominated by the magnificent collegiate church of the Holy Trinity, and has probably changed little since Katherine saw it five centuries ago.

19. Thomas Cranmer,
Henry VIII's Archbishop
of Canterbury, by
Gerlach Flicke (1545).
One of the principal
architects of the
Reformation in England,
he paid the ultimate
penalty when the
Catholic Mary became
queen.

20. Thomas Cromwell,
King Henry's chief
minister in the 1530s.
Widely believed to have
engineered Anne Boleyn's
downfall, he was himself
executed in 1540.

Right: 21. The title page of the Great Bible, Henry VIII's Bible in English, which became required reading in every parish in 1538. The king is shown as Head of the Church in England dispensing divine truth to Archbishop Cranmer and the clergy on his right, and Thomas Cromwell and the laity on his left.

Below: 22. Grimsthorpe Castle. Sir John Vanburgh's baroque north front, built in the early eighteenth century. It replaced the seventeenth-century classical front which had itself replaced Charles Brandon's building work.

23. Grimsthorpe Castle. The Bertie arms, three battering 'rams' (note the rams' heads) supported by a hermit (held to represent 'good') and a wild man ('evil'), adorn the entrance gates to the north front.

24. Grimsthorpe Castle. The south range still retains its Tudor ambience, although it has been altered by the addition of gables and the insertion of later windows. The re-faced King John's Tower, the oldest part of the castle, stands in the south-east corner, on the extreme right of the picture.

Above: 25. These pieces of carved limestone, which may have formed part of an archway or a decorative pillar, are the small remains of Vaudey Abbey, a Cistercian monastery that stood just south of the lake at Grimsthorpe. Charles Brandon used much of the fabric to rebuild the castle in *c.* 1540.

Right: 26. Henry VIII in later life, when his relationship with Katherine developed. Drawn by E. L. Wedgwood from a carving in boxwood, by Holbein, at Sudeley Castle.

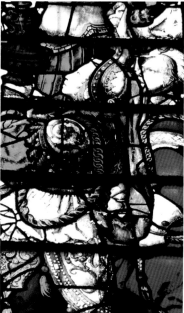

Above left: 27. Anne of Cleves in the portrait by Holbein which helped to persuade King Henry to marry her. Katherine was among those who welcomed her to England and became one of the 'great ladies' of her household. *Above right:* 29. Catherine Howard, the second of Henry's wives to go to the block. This detail from the window depicting King Solomon and the Queen of Sheba in King's College Chapel, Cambridge is believed to be modelled on her. *Bottom:* 28. 'Anne of Cleves House' at Lewes (Sussex), one of the properties Anne received as part of her divorce settlement. The fates of Catherine of Aragon, Anne Boleyn and Catherine Howard must have weighed heavily on Katherine Willoughby when she realised that Henry VIII might wish to marry her, but Anne of Cleves's generous settlement showed that the relationship did not always have to end badly.

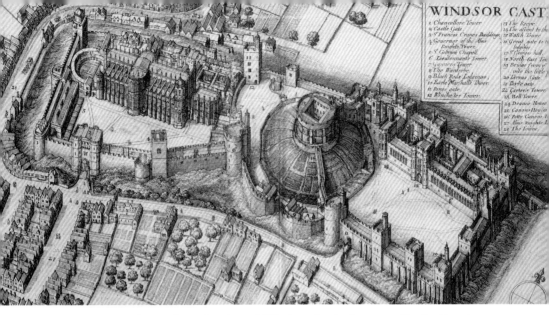

30. Wenceslas Hollar's drawing of Windsor Castle. In 1545 Charles Brandon, Katherine's first husband, was buried here in St George's Chapel (no. 5 in the key), at Henry VIII's request.

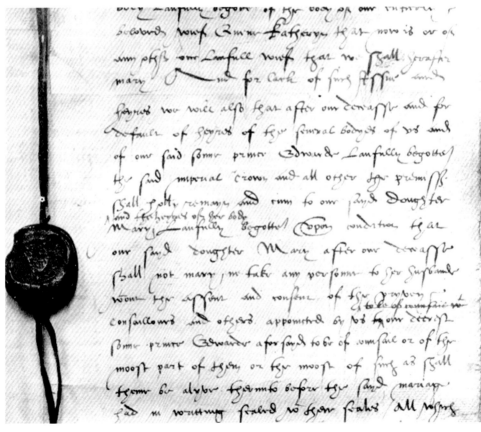

31. Henry VIII's will. A king's authority died with him, and Henry's efforts to determine the succession succeeded only because the Lady Jane Grey plot failed.

Above: 32. Catherine Parr, Katherine's friend and fellow Protestant. Her grave was rediscovered in the ruined chapel at Sudeley Castle (Glos.) in the 1780s, and fifty years later the architect Sir George Gilbert Scott designed this altar tomb and effigy 'rendered as correctly as it could be from the portraits which are now extant'.

Left: 33. The tomb of Catherine Parr (detail).

Right: 34. Edward, Prince of Wales, the future Edward VI, captured by Holbein in 1542 when he would have been about five years old. Katherine and her friends anticipated a Protestant utopia when he succeeded, but it was not to last long.

Below: 35. The coronation procession of Edward VI in February, 1547. Katherine's two sons by Charles Brandon, Henry and Charles, were admitted to the order of the Bath on this occasion, and Henry carried the orb.

Edward Prince of Wales.

11. PRINZ EDWARD VON WALES, VORSTUDIE ZUM BILDNIS VON 1542.

Opposite top: 36. St John's College, Cambridge, where Katherine's sons studied. The statue over the gateway of the second court, built 1598-1602, is of Bess of Hardwick (who paid for the construction), and beneath are her arms flanked by the Tudor rose (left), and the Beaufort portcullis (right).

Opposite bottom: 37. Edward Seymour, Duke of Somerset, Queen Jane's brother and Edward VI's first Protector. Katherine wanted to aid him when he was threatened with execution, but feared her intervention would do more harm than good.

Top: 38. Thomas Seymour, Baron Sudeley, Somerset's jealous younger brother and Catherine Parr's last husband. Katherine reluctantly cared for his daughter after his mad scheme to kidnap Edward VI brought him to the block.

Bottom: 39. William Parr, Marquis of Northampton, Queen Catherine's brother. He declined to help Katherine support his late sister's orphaned child.

Left: 40. Lady Jane Grey, Katherine's step-granddaughter, a nineteenth-century portrait in stained glass in the chapel of Sudeley Castle. Jane acted as chief mourner at Catherine Parr's funeral.

Above: 41. Map of Whitehall and Westminster. The Lady Jane Grey conspirators were tried in Westminster Hall, and Katherine's step-daughter Frances and step-granddaughter Mary were both buried in the Abbey.

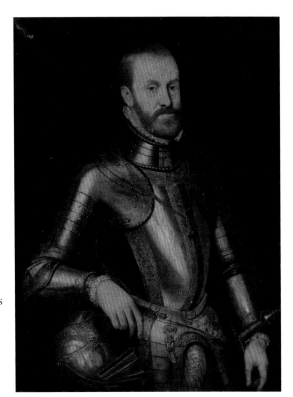

42. Queen Mary's husband, King Philip II of Spain. Mary's decision to marry Philip provoked an uprising which resulted in the executions of Lady Jane, her husband Guildford, and her father the Duke of Suffolk.

43. Hugh Latimer, Katherine's principal spiritual mentor, portrayed adoring the crucified Christ, in a modern stained glass window in the chapel of Clare College, Cambridge. The figure wearing red is the Protestant scholar and courtier Nicholas Ferrar (1592-1637). Both he and Latimer were Fellows of Clare.

A table deſcribing the burning of Biſhop Ridley and Father Latimer at Oxford, D.Smith there preaching at the time of their martirdome.

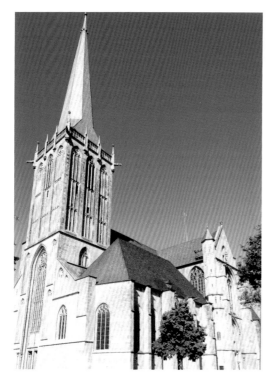

Above: 44. The burning of Hugh Latimer and Nicholas Ridley in Oxford on 16 October 1555. The now exiled Katherine had listened to many of Latimer's sermons and sent money to Ridley in prison.

Left: 45. St Willibrord's Church Wesel, where Katherine sought sanctuary during her flight from England in 1555.

46. Windeck Castle, Weinheim, where Katherine lived from April 1556 to April 1557. John Brett climbed the hill to deliver Queen Mary's letters, but was forced to beat a hasty retreat.

47. A drawing of a more mature Katherine by George Vertue (1684-1756), now at Sudeley Castle. The legend on the reverse reads 'Catherine Willoughby Duchess of Suffolk, fourth wife of Charles Brandon, copied by Vertue from the original by Holbein at Kensington' (see Appendix 2).

48. Queen Elizabeth I by an unknown artist. Katherine and the Queen were both devout Protestants, but they did not always see eye to eye.

49. Lucas de Heere's *An Allegory of the Tudor Succession*, painted around 1572. On Henry VIII's left are Edward VI and Queen Elizabeth, and on his right Queen Mary and her husband Philip of Spain. Behind Elizabeth are 'Peace' and 'Plenty', and behind Philip Mars, the God of War.

50. The tomb of Katherine's friend and confidant William Cecil, Lord Burghley, in St Martin's church, Stamford.

[The inscription, contained within three panels, two on the south (Chancel) side and one on the north (Chapel) side of the monument reads (in translation):

'Sacred to God most good and great, and to memory. The most honourable and far renowned Lord William Cecil, Baron of Burghley, Lord High Treasurer of England, President of the Court of Wards, knight of the most noble order of the Garter, Privy Counsellor to the most serene Elizabeth, Queen of England, &c., and Chancellor of the University of Cambridge, under this tomb awaits the second coming of Christ.

Who for the excellent endowments of his mind, was first made Privy Counsellor to Edward the sixth, King of England; afterwards to Queen Elizabeth: under whom being intrusted with the greatest and most weighty affairs of this kingdom, and above all others approved, in promoting the true religion, and providing for the safety and honour of the commonwealth; by his prudence, honesty, integrity, and great services to the nation, he obtained the highest honours: and when he had lived long enough to nature, long enough to glory, but not long enough to his country, quietly fell asleep in Christ.

He had two wives: Mary, sister of Sir John Cheeke, knight, of whom he begat one son, Thomas, now Baron of Burghley; and Mildred, daughter of Sir Anthony Cooke, knight, who bore to him Sir Robert Cecil, knight, Privy Counsellor to Queen Elizabeth and President of the Court of Wards; Anne, married to Edward, Earl of Oxford; and Elizabeth to William Wentworth, eldest son of Baron Wentworth.']

Above: 51. William Cecil's tomb (detail).

Left: 52. Robert Dudley, Earl of Leicester, in old age. Dudley avoided serious punishment for his part in the Lady Jane Grey conspiracy and later, became Queen Elizabeth's great favourite. Katherine appealed to him when she feared Elizabeth was about to have her executed.

53. Katherine and Richard Bertie's monument at St James's Church, Spilsby, Lincolnshire, occupies the western end of the Willoughby chapel, the chancel of the pre-1350 building. The base is inscribed 'Sepulchrum D. Ricardi Bertie et D. Catherinae Ducissae Suffolkiae, Baronissae de Wylughby et Eresby, conivgv. ista obit xix Septemb. 1580 Ille obit ix Aprilis, 1582', and the three figures supporting heraldic shields represent (from left to right) a hermit (part of the Willoughby coat of arms), a Saracen king (attribution uncertain) and a wild man (Ufford).

54 & 55. The alabaster busts of Katherine Willoughby and Richard Bertie are more finely carved than the rest of the structure, and are disproportionate to the tall niches in which they sit. It is possible that they were originally made to be displayed elsewhere.

56. The back (western-facing) side of the monument is inscribed with five biblical quotations (in Latin) from Job, Hebrews, and the Gospels of Luke and John, all concerned with the coming judgement and the hope of salvation. The sixth (illustrated) is an English rhyme observing that everyone is equal in death.

57. Inscribed stone set into the building formerly occupied by the King Edward VI Grammar School at Spilsby. The school was founded by royal charter and endowed by Katherine in November 1550.

58. Part of the London skyline by Claes Visscher. Visscher painted this in 1616, more than three decades after Katherine's death, but the scene would have changed little in the intervening years. Complete, it is more than two metres long.

59. Greenwich Palace and London from Greenwich Hill, from a contemporary drawing by Anthonis van den Wyngaerde. The palace was one of Henry VIII's favourite residences, and Katherine knew it well.

60. The White Tower of the Tower of London, from a mid- fifteenth century illumination. Katherine's step-granddaughters Jane and Catherine Grey and her friends Anne Askew, William Cecil, Hugh Latimer and Protector Somerset were all imprisoned in the complex at different times.

61. The White Tower as it appears today.

62. St Michael and All Angels' church, Edenham (Lincs) replaced Spilsby as the Willoughby family mausoleum in the seventeenth century. Many of Katherine's descendants are buried here and their memorials are to be found both within the building and in the cemetery to the east.

63. Edenham Church. Memorial tablet to Lady Cecilie Goff, Katherine's first biographer, who died in 1960.

64. The Willoughby Arms, Little Bytham. In the mid-nineteenth century the family built their own private railway connecting Grimsthorpe and Edenham with the Great Northern Railway at Little Bytham.

Right: 65. Katherine Willoughby, Duchess of Suffolk, a miniature after Holbein showing her as a young woman. (Private collection)

Below: 66. An old postcard of Parham Hall, Suffolk, where Katherine was born in 1519. Pevsner calls it a 'wonderful' example of a moated early sixteenth-century timber-framed house.

Parham Hall. Suffolk, 1815.

67. Two bosses from the Lady chapel of Southwold Church, Suffolk, said by an old postcard to represent Charles Brandon and Mary Tudor, although the style of the man's beard and the woman's headdress are earlier. They may have lived at Henham, near Southwold, for a time after Henry VIII 'forgave' their impulsive marriage. (Geoffrey Wheeler)

68. Suffolk Place, Charles Brandon's town house on the west side of Borough High Street in Southwark, a detail from Wyngearde's panorama of London around 1550. It was a 'large and sumptuous house' (Stow) surmounted by polygonal turrets and cupolas, but in 1536 the king obliged Brandon to exchange it for the Bishop of Norwich's house near Charing Cross.

69. After Charles Brandon took up residence in Lincolnshire he converted the thirteenth-century fortress at Grimsthorpe into a modern, comfortable dwelling. This engraving by Kip shows the house as it appeared in 1674.

70. The burning of Anne Askew and others, 15 July 1546, from John Foxe's *Acts and Monuments*. She was convicted of heresy under Henry VIII's 1539 Act of Six Articles, which had made denying the real presence of Christ in the sacrament a capital offence, and became the first Protestant to be executed for her religious beliefs. She knew both Catherine Parr and Katherine Willoughby, and was tortured by religious conservatives in an unsuccessful attempt to obtain evidence against those who shared her views.

71. Henry VIII in old age, posthumous engraving by Cornelis Metsys, redrawn by Geoffrey Wheeler. Of all the pictures of the king, this one may best portray him at the time he was romantically linked to Katherine Willoughby.

72. Martin Bucer, from Foxe's *Acts and Monuments*. Katherine enjoyed a close, albeit brief, friendship with Bucer after he was appointed Regius Professor of Divinity at Cambridge, and is said to have helped nurse him in his last illness.

MARTIN BUCER.

73. Stephen Gardiner, Bishop of Winchester, had been Katherine's friend when they were both committed to the 'old' religion, but their relationship deteriorated badly after she became a Protestant.

My deuise for the Succession.

For lakke of issu of my body...

Above: 74. Hugh Latimer preaching before Edward VI from the 'preaching place', the pulpit Henry VIII had built in the palace garden at Whitehall. From Foxe's *Acts and Monuments.*

Left: 75. Edward VI's 'Device for the Succession' composed entirely in his own handwriting, naming Lady Jane Grey his heir. The original designation 'to the Lady Jane's heirs male' has been amended to read 'to the Lady Jane and her heirs male'. (Jonathan Reeve CD 2 b20p987 15001550)

76. Myles Coverdale. Best known for his translation of the Bible, he aided Katherine during her exile and lived in her house for almost five years after their return to England.

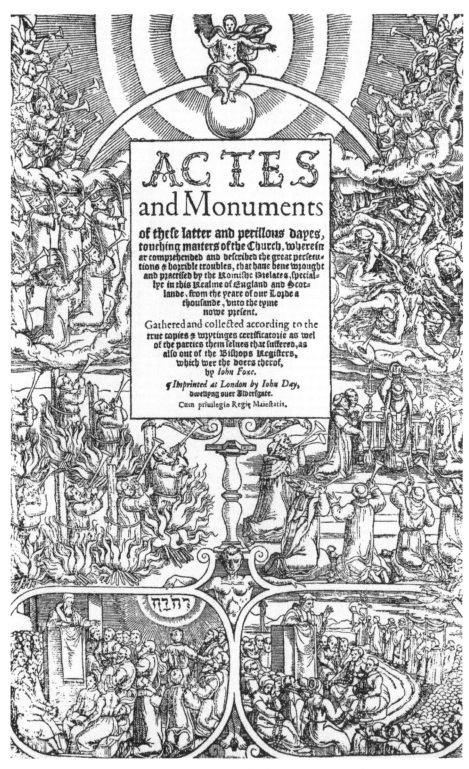

77. Title page from the first (1563) edition of John Foxe's *Acts and Monuments* or *Book of Martyrs*. Katherine never became a martyr, but was still considered a heroine of the Protestant cause.

78. Richard Bertie,
Katherine's second
husband, from a picture
by Holbein painted in
1548 when he had just
turned thirty. From
Georgina Bertie, *Five
Generations of a Loyal
House part 1* (1845).

79. Peregrine Bertie,
Lord Willoughby,
Katherine's only surviving
son, 'in the dress of the
Low Countries'. From
Georgina Bertie, *Five
Generations of a Loyal
House part 1* (1845).

80. Suzan Bertie, Katherine's only daughter. A portrait by 'the Master of the Countess of Warwick' dated to 1567, when she would have been about thirteen.

81. The arms of Bertie, Willoughby, Beke and Ufford, from Georgina Bertie, *Five Generations of a Loyal House part 1* (1845). Note how they have been incorporated into the design of Katherine and Richard Bertie's monument at Spilsby.

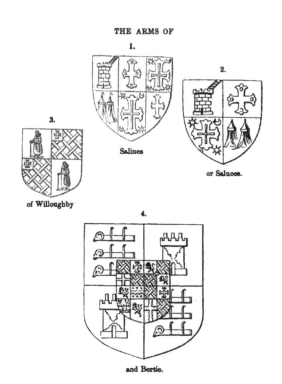

82. Katherine and Richard Bertie's arms 'with the crest of the Uffords, Earls of Suffolk'. From Georgina Bertie, *Five Generations of a Loyal House part 1* (1845).

attendance in a non-belligerent albeit still formal manner, but instead instructed the Sheriff of Lincolnshire 'to attach [arrest] the said Richard immediately, and without bail bring him up to London'. The sheriff clearly thought this unnecessary and accepted his bond 'with two sureties in a thousand pounds' that he would present himself before Gardiner on 23 March 1554 (Good Friday); but when he arrived at the chancellor's house 'by St Mary Overy's' he was brusquely told that the latter was too preoccupied with his devotions to interview him. Gardiner finally appeared for a few moments, but only to accuse Bertie of ignoring two previous subpoenas (of which he knew nothing), and threatening 'to make him an example to all Lincolnshire for his obstinacy'.

Bertie asked Gardiner to 'suspend his displeasure' until the matter had been investigated, whereupon the chancellor ordered him not to depart without leave and to wait upon him again the next morning 'at seven of the clock'. When he did so he found that he was no longer accused of ignoring the earlier summonses – perhaps Gardiner had discovered his error – but it was put to him that Charles Brandon had owed the Crown £4,000 for which Katherine, as his executor, was responsible. Bertie protested that the debt had been 'estalled and truly answered', i.e. settled in instalments, in Edward VI's reign under terms agreed with the king's father, and Gardiner promised that 'if it be true that you say, I will show you favour'. But now he turned to what was almost certainly the real reason for their meeting, the question of religion. He did not, he claimed, doubt Bertie, 'whose mother I know to be as godly and catholic as any within this land', but Katherine was a different matter. He rehearsed the occasions when she had slighted him – when she had named her dog after him and dressed it in a rochet, when she had chosen him as the man she loved worst to escort her into dinner, and when she had referred to him as the 'wolf' whose imprisonment made the Protestant 'lambs' safer – and asked Bertie sarcastically if she 'was now as ready to set up the Mass, as she was lately to pull it down'.

Bertie made what excuses he could. Her words, he said, 'though in that season they sounded bitter to your lordship, yet if it would please you without offence to know the cause, I am sure the one will purge the other'. In the matter of the dog he protested that 'she was neither the author, nor the allower'; but he was astute enough to recognise that it was not so much these old quarrels which troubled Gardiner as Katherine's attitude towards the old religion and the new order. He cautiously pointed out that the reformed faith had held sway in England in King Edward's reign, and argued that while coercion could force individuals to pay lip service to Catholicism their minds would only be changed by persuasion. Gardiner asked him bluntly if he thought Katherine could be persuaded to alter her opinions – to which Bertie replied, perhaps with less than complete honesty, 'Yea, verily ... for she is reasonable enough.' With that he dismissed him, observing wryly that 'it will be a marvellous grief to the prince of Spain, and to all the nobility that shall come with him, when they shall find but two noble personages of the Spanish race within this land, the queen and my lady your wife; and one of them gone from the faith'.[3]

The content of these meetings between Bertie and Gardiner (and virtually the entire story of Katherine's escape and exile), has been preserved by the Protestant martyrologist John Foxe, whose *Acts and Monuments* was first published in 1563. Foxe cannot be regarded as a wholly reliable source of information, not least because much of the research and writing of his great work was undertaken by others; but he knew Latimer and

Cecil, who partially funded him, and stayed with Katherine (or possibly with her stepdaughter Frances) before he was ordained deacon by Nicholas Ridley in 1550. It is likely therefore, that in this case he obtained some of his material personally and at first hand, but his aim was always to emphasise how much his subjects had suffered for their faith rather than to minimise it. Even if he heard the gist of Bertie's conversations with Gardiner directly from the former he was not standing at his elbow with a shorthand notepad; and other possible exaggerations will be noted as our story unfolds.[4]

Bertie returned home to Katherine and Suzan, not a little troubled and deep in thought. Gardiner had seemed ready to accept his explanations and assurances, but was he merely biding his time? Bertie knew that Katherine had recently sent Latimer and Ridley money to ease the rigours of their imprisonment, and feared that, if this was discovered, it would result in their own arrest and condemnation. The two clergymen were cautious after a fashion. Ridley made no mention of the gift when he wrote to Katherine, but in another letter asked Augustine Bernher to thank her in person:

Brother Augustine ... I have received my lady's grace's alms, six royals [ryalls], six shillings and eight pence. I have written a letter here unto her grace, but I have made no mention thereof; wherefore I desire you to render her grace hearty thanks. Blessed be God, as for myself, I want nothing, but my lady's alms cometh happily to relieve my poor brother's [Latimer's] necessity ... Read my letter to my lady's grace. I would Mistress [Joan] Wilkinson and Mrs [Anne] Warcup had a copy of it; for although the letter is directed to my lady's grace alone, yet the matter thereof pertaineth indifferently [equally] to her grace and to all good women which love God and His word in deed and truth. Yours in Christ, N.R.

Again, Ridley did not name the 'lady's grace' he wished to thank, but another hand has added, 'This alms was sent him by the Lady Catherine Duchess of Suffolk, to whom again he wrote again a worthy letter, which is lost, and many other written both to her and others'.[5]

It seemed clear to Katherine and Bertie that it would only be a matter of time before they were themselves arrested or before the government demanded an unacceptable degree of religious conformity, and they decided to seek liberty in flight. Their plan was that Bertie should first go to Protestant Europe to see what arrangements he could make for them, but how could he leave England without arousing suspicion? His solution was to propose to Gardiner that he should seek to recover sums of money still owed to Charles Brandon's estate by a number of Continental debtors, one of whom was the Emperor. Gardiner suggested that it would be better to wait until Philip (the Emperor's son) had married Queen Mary, but Bertie argued that, on the contrary, the Emperor would be less likely to settle the matter once the marriage had taken place and he had obtained everything he wanted. Gardiner saw the sense of this reasoning, and a few days later Bertie received a royal licence 'not only to pass the seas, but to pass and repass them so often as to him seemed good, till he had finished all his business and causes beyond the seas'.[6]

Bertie left England in June 1554. It is unclear if he returned at intervals during the remainder of the year, but at some point Katherine moved from Grimsthorpe to the Barbican, her London town house, in readiness for her escape.[7] They confided their plans to a trusted friend 'an old gentleman [servant] called master Robert Cranwell, whom master Berty had specially provided for that purpose', and on New Year's Day, 'betwixt four and five of the clock in the morning', Katherine emerged into the chill darkness carrying little Suzan in her arms. She was dressed as a merchant's wife and was accompanied by Cranwell and six servants who had been told of her plans only at the last moment – Foxe says they had been chosen for their 'meanness ... for she doubted the best would not adventure that fortune with her'. They were a gentlewoman (the same Margaret Blakborn who had been her sons' governess and who hardly fits Foxe's description), a laundress, and four men, 'one a Greek born which was a rider of horses, another a joiner, the third a brewer [and] the fourth a fool, one of the kitchen'.

Their leaving was not without incident. The inevitable hustle and bustle roused a man named Atkinson, whom Foxe describes as 'a herald, keeper of her [Katherine's] house' who came to investigate. Whoever Atkinson was, Katherine did not trust him, and in her haste was compelled to leave behind a 'mail' (a pack or bag) containing clothes for her daughter and 'a milk-pot with milk'. She quickly ordered the five men with her to go ahead to Lion Quay, between London Bridge and Billingsgate, from where they intended to set sail, while she and her two women concealed themselves in the shadows of the nearby Charterhouse. Atkinson peered out from the gate of the Barbican, saw nothing but the abandoned 'mail', and decided to take it back into the house to investigate its contents. Katherine breathed a sigh of relief and began her journey into the unknown.[8]

The first problem they encountered was that neither Katherine nor her women knew how to reach their intended destination. But they had a stroke of good fortune. Foxe says that 'she [Katherine] took the way that led to Finsbury-field, and the others walked the city streets as they lay open before them, till by chance, more than discretion, they met all suddenly together a little within Moorgate, from whence they passed directly to Lion-quay'. They found the barge that Cranwell had arranged would transport them, and after persuading the reluctant steersman to 'launch out on a morning so misty', reached Leigh, below Tilbury, later that day.[9]

At Leigh, Cranwell arranged for Katherine to stay with a friend, a London merchant named William Gosling who had a married daughter who was not known in the area. Gosling simply informed the curious that his 'daughter' had come to pay him a visit, and Katherine took the opportunity to replace the necessities she had left behind at the Barbican. What arrangements had been made to accommodate the other members of the party is not stated, but at some point Bertie made his appearance and was reunited with his wife. Foxe says that they were obliged to spend their last night in England at an inn in the town, where they were 'again almost betrayed, yet notwithstanding, by God's good working she escaped that hazard'.[10]

It is not entirely clear how long the couple had to wait before safe passage could be found for them. Logically, they would not have delayed a moment longer than necessary, but Lady Goff mentions 'an account of the inquisition that was taken in Kent of their goods and chattels [in which] it is stated that Bertie and the duchess sailed in the same ship from Gravesend on the fifth of February, 1555'.[11] Three times they set sail and twice were carried 'almost into the coast of Zealand' before contrary winds forced them back to England. 'And at the last [second] recoil, certain persons came to the shore, suspecting that she [Katherine] was within that ship; yet having examined one of her company that was a-land for fresh achates [provisions], and finding, by the simplicity of his tale, only the appearance of a mean merchant's wife to be a-shipboard, [they] ceased any further search.'[12]

Foxe's theme throughout his narrative is that Katherine stood in constant danger of arrest and punishment, but this is not altogether consistent with the known facts. He notes that after she fled the Barbican 'as soon as the day permitted, the council was informed of her departure; and some of them [the councillors] came forth to her house, to inquire of the manner thereof, and took an inventory of her goods'. An order to 'search and watch to apprehend and stay her' was issued, but this may have been no more than a formality, or gesture on the part of the government. Mary had been queen for a full eighteen months when Katherine and Bertie made their bid for freedom, and anyone charged with keeping them under surveillance could have discerned their intentions. News of the sale of their furniture at Grimsthorpe had circulated in Lincolnshire and London, and Katherine had not hesitated to share her plans with those closest to her. A trusted servant had been charged to administer their estates in their absence, and they had made no attempt to encourage Gardiner to believe that they would reconvert to Catholicism. On the contrary, Bertie had written to him defending the couple's shared commitment to evangelicalism, and informed him that he would support his wife in her faith as 'all the rest in her I love, embrace, and honour even unto the grave'.[13]

The implication then is that the Marian government suspected, even knew, that Katherine and her husband were planning to go into exile but did not seriously try to prevent them. It was impossible to burn or even imprison everyone who held Protestant opinions, and Queen Mary would have been mindful of the sacrifices Maria de Salinas had made for her own mother. If

Katherine had remained in England she would have been at best an irritation or at worst a focus for opposition; but in Europe she would be out of sight and largely out of mind. It is worth repeating that Foxe wanted to emphasise his subjects' courage and the difficulties they experienced (a theme which, as we will see, he maintained throughout his account of Katherine's exile), but it is likely that Gardiner and others felt more relief than frustration when they learned she had finally 'escaped'.

7

EXILE
1555–1559

Foxe says that 'so soon as the duchess had landed in Brabant, she and her women were apparelled like the women of the Netherlands with hukes [long hooded cloaks]; and so she and her husband took their journey towards Cleveland [the Duchy of Cleves, in the Holy Roman Empire], and being arrived at a town therein called Santon [modern Xanten], took a house there, until they might further devise of some sure place, where to settle themselves'.[1] They hoped to find permanent refuge in Wesel, another of the Duke of Cleves's towns some eleven miles distant, 'wither divers Walloons[2] were fled for [their] religion and had for their minister one Francis Perusell, then called Francis de Rivers, who had received some courtesy in England at the duchess's hands'.[3] Through Perusell, Bertie asked the Wesel authorities to grant them a permit of residence, and Foxe implies that he obtained it the more readily because the chief magistrate knew who they really were.

But even while their application was being considered their presence in Santon aroused suspicion. It was rumoured that they 'were greater personages than they gave themselves forth' i.e. than they were pretending to be, and Bertie was warned that the Bishop of Arras, Antoine de Perrault, was planning to question them about their reasons for being there and their religious opinions. They decided that they must leave for Wesel immediately, and one cold February afternoon, 'about three of the clock', set out on foot 'without hiring of horse or waggon for fear of disclosing their purpose'. They took only two servants with them, and again carried baby Suzan in their arms.[4]

Their journey was far from easy. In the late afternoon 'there fell a mighty rain of continuance, whereby a long frost and ice, before congealed, was thawed, which doubled more their weariness'. As darkness fell, they sent their servants into the villages they passed to attempt to hire a cart or other conveyance, but none was available and they were obliged to struggle on as best they could. They reached Wesel at between the hours of six and seven, but Bertie did not know where to find Perusell and could obtain no shelter for his family. 'For going from inn to inn offering large money for small lodging, they were refused of all the inn-holders, suspecting Berty to be a lance-knight [landsknecht],[5] and the duchess to be his woman. The child for cold and sustenance cried pitifully; the mother wept as fast; [and] the heavens rained as fast as the clouds could pour.'[6]

With their situation becoming ever more desperate, Bertie left the others in the porch of St Willibrord's church while he tried to find someone who could direct him to Master Perusell's dwelling. He supposed his fluency in French, Italian and Latin would stand him in good stead, but found that none of the locals he approached could understand him. Finally, when he had almost given up hope, he overheard two boys speaking Latin, and offered to reward them if they would take him and his family 'to some Walloon's house'. By chance, they led them to the very house where Perusell happened to be dining that evening, and when he came to the door 'beholding master Berty, the duchess, and their child, their faces, apparels, and bodies so far from their old form, deformed with dirt, weather, and heaviness, [he] could not speak to them, nor they to him, for tears. At length recovering themselves, they saluted one another, and so together entered the house, God knoweth full joyfully; master Berty changing his apparel with the good man [the householder], the duchess with the good wife, and their child with the child of the house.'[7]

Perusell was able to tell Katherine and Bertie that he had obtained permission for them to settle in Wesel, and with his help 'within a few days after' they rented 'a very fair house in the town'. It was either now – or perhaps, as Evelyn Read suggests, just before they fled into the late afternoon twilight – that Katherine was able to tell her husband that, at the age of thirty-six, she was again pregnant. It goes without saying that if Bertie was aware of his wife's condition when they left Santon his concern for her well-being would have been still greater.[8] There are too many unknowns to arrive at anything like a reliable estimate, but Katherine would arguably have conceived between 20 and 28 January, between 257 and 265 days before her son Peregrine (so called for their travels, or peregrinations), was born on 12 October.[9] If she and her family did not make their escape until near the end of February she may well have detected the first signs of pregnancy, but it is a tight time frame. Foxe could have learned this from Richard Bertie, or merely seized upon it as a means of adding more pathos to an already pitiful tale.

Foxe clearly delighted in emphasising, perhaps even exaggerating, his subjects' sufferings, and there are some other aspects of his description of this first phase of Katherine's exile that are puzzling and not wholly believable. It is unclear why Bertie did not ask Perusell to help them find sanctuary in Wesel until they reached Santon (it is a poor reflection on the six months he had allegedly spent making arrangements for them to settle on the Continent), and we can only wonder why he did not try to meet him in person. Why, at some point, did he not ride or walk the eleven miles from Santon to discover where their friend lived and how their application to reside in Wesel was progressing? And why did they go from inn to inn seeking shelter when they knew his name and presumably his address? Letters were sometimes entrusted to carriers and left at a place the recipient was known to visit, but again, we are left with the impression that a little forethought would have smoothed their path considerably. It is, of course, possible that Bertie *had* done some or all of these things, but that making him appear dilatory and at times hapless added greatly to the drama of Foxe's account.

Foxe also has the story that 'it was by this time [common knowledge] throughout the whole town what discourtesy the inn-holders had showed unto them [the family] at their entry, insomuch that on the Sunday following, a preacher in the pulpit openly, and in sharp terms, rebuked that great incivility towards strangers, by allegation of sundry places out of holy Scriptures, discoursing how not only princes sometimes are received in the image of private persons, but angels in the shape of men'. Again, it is possible to allow that something of this sort actually happened, but Katherine and Bertie, who had always tried to avoid attracting attention in each place where they had sought refuge, would surely have wished he had spoken otherwise. The last thing they wanted was to have their whereabouts shouted from the rooftops – even if the shouter was on their side![10]

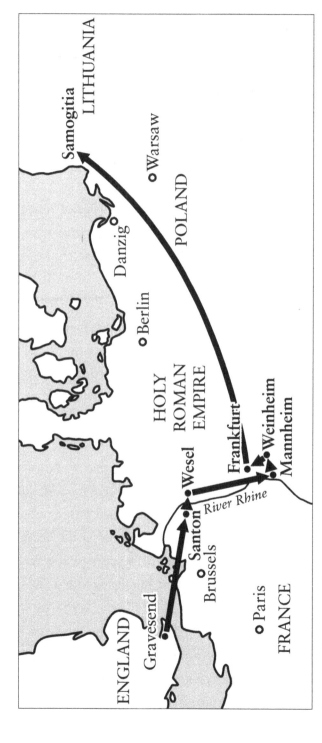

Map of Katherine's travels in Europe 1555–1557, drawn by Thomas Bohm after Geoffrey Wheeler.

Foxe does not say how long the Berties lived in Wesel, but his statement that they still had only one child born to them when they were obliged to move again is not supported by other evidence. The contemporary register records that Peregrine was baptised in 'our church in the suburbs, called Upper Mathem, by Hen. Bonichus, minister', on 14 October, and his birth in the town was reportedly commemorated by the erection of no fewer than two 'monuments' in St Willibrord's eastern porch. Lady Goff reports that the first of these 'having been defaced by the destroying hand of time and by military violence, one of his [Peregrine's] descendants who visited Germany as Royal Ambassador toward the close of the reign of Charles II, in veneration of his memory, and proud of ancestors, who had been honoured to suffer exile for the Protestant Religion, caused another stone to be substituted in its place bearing an appropriate inscription'.[11] The joy Katherine and her husband felt at the birth of a son would have been tempered by the news that Hugh Latimer had been burned at the stake in Oxford only two days after the baptism, and they are unlikely to have drawn much comfort from Bishop Gardiner's death a month later.

At some point during the winter of 1555/6 they were warned by Sir John Mason – Queen Mary's ambassador to the Netherlands no less – that they were again in danger. Lord Paget, who as Sir William Paget had stood surety for Katherine after the death of her first husband and was now the Queen's Keeper of the Seals, had 'feigned an errand to the baths' that would bring him to Wesel, and had arranged for the Duke of Brunswick 'who was shortly with ten ensigns[12] to pass by Wesel for the service of the house of Austria against the French king', to take the Berties into custody. They decided, says Foxe, to seek refuge in the Palatinate, ruled then by the staunchly Protestant Prince-Elector Otto Heinrich. Otto and his late brother had been on friendly terms with Martin Bucer, and they felt sure he would welcome them there.

This may be only part of the story, however. The Berties' presence in Wesel had encouraged other fugitives from Marian England to join the exile community in the town, and before long they numbered nearly a hundred. In October 1555 they acquired a building in which they could meet separately; but the city fathers, who were committed to the tenets of the Lutheran statement of faith, the 'Confession of Augsburg', would not allow them to celebrate communion after their own manner. The exiles saw no merit in attending services conducted in a language they did not understand and which still retained what, in their view, were elements of popery, and a further clash led to the revocation of their permit to worship independently. Melissa Harkrider says that 'Willoughby and other English exiles left Wesel rather than compromise', and it is likely that the ban influenced their decision to some extent.[13]

Foxe says that they decided to go to Windsheim, but he was perhaps confusing unfamiliar place names. Their destination was Weinheim in the Odenwald, not (Bad) Windsheim in Bavaria some 85 miles to the east. He says nothing about their journey, but an almost 200-mile voyage up the Rhine as far as Mannheim, undertaken in winter with two small children, would have taxed all their resources. Mannheim is only a dozen miles from Weinheim, but it would still have been necessary to hire horses and a cart to reach their destination. It must have been a tired, somewhat bedraggled group of travellers who, in April 1556, finally arrived at what they hoped would become their new, permanent home.

Weinheim, writes Mrs Read, lay 'in a curve of the mountains protected from the cold north-east winds, and had a warm, gentle climate. Citron grew there, and even some dwarf palms; but beech trees and occasional oaks reminded the Berties of Lincolnshire and here and there a field of grain waved on the steep hillsides.' Myles Coverdale, the Bible translator who had been the Wesel community's first minister and who was now living in the Palatinate, had contacted the prince-elector on their behalf, and with his help 'the little family settled down in a castle [Windeck] high on a hill by the town, a castle with thick walls and gates'. The grant of the place included household provisions, hunting rights, and the services of Christopher Landschade, the resident steward.[14]

Katherine and her husband had put more miles between themselves and Queen Mary's England, but found that, even here, they were not entirely beyond the government's reach. In July 1556 one John Brett arrived in the town bearing what were almost certainly warrants ordering the couple to return immediately to England. 'I went up the hill a good half English mile high,' he tells us, '[but] when I came before the castle gates I found them fast shut and a stripling like an English lackey standing before them. Of him I demanded if the said duchess and Bertie were within.' The 'lackey' confirmed that this was the case, demanded to know Brett's name and business, and told him to remain where he was while he informed his master and mistress. After waiting for a short time Brett and his attendant heard the noise of stones being moved in the window of a turret over the gate, and looking up saw two men who began to shout 'kill them, kill them' in French. A missile lobbed from above narrowly missed Brett's head, injuring his hand, and before he could recover himself some of Katherine's servants rushed from the gateway 'with great fierceness', forcing him to retire down the hill. His assailants followed him into the town where the noise of their shouts soon attracted a crowd of onlookers. 'The Englishmen,' he writes, 'cried to move the people against me and my man [saying] that we were thieves and papists come into those parts with purpose to carry away the duchess their lady or by some secret means to poison her and their master, favourers of the Gospel and truth.' He won breathing space by protesting that his errand 'was not to the confusion of their lady as they alleged but rather to her singular comfort', but could not prevent his attackers from stealing his horses from the inn where he was lodging and taking them up to the castle.

A senior local official whom Brett calls a Kelder now appeared on the scene and both parties repeated their arguments, Brett maintaining that he meant Katherine no harm and that delivering letters from the Queen of England to two of her subjects did not diminish the prince-elector's authority in his own country. The Kelder ordered that Brett and his servant should be detained at their inn until he had learned Katherine's 'pleasure' in the matter (clearly, he was aware that she stood high in Otto-Heinrich's favour), and when he returned brought with him William Barlow, the deprived Bishop of Bath and Wells who acted as her chaplain, and 'three or four' others. Barlow claimed the Berties were unhappy with their servants' behaviour, and asked Brett if the letters he carried were 'missives' (i.e. unthreatening), in which case they would consent to receive them, or 'process', instructions they could not lawfully disregard. Brett refused to divulge the contents, so Barlow appealed to the Kelder who insisted that they could only be delivered with the approval of another official, the Palsgrave.[15] Procrastination seemed useless, so Brett, anxious to avoid being 'ryffled' by Barlow and those with him, handed the documents to the Kelder on the understanding that they would not be opened or shown to anyone unless he was present. He was then again confined to his inn where, he tells us, he was 'very evil entreated and lodged'.

Five days later the Palsgrave sent two men at arms with instructions to bring Brett to Heidelberg, the capital of the Palatinate, some fifteen miles distant. Before he left his letters were returned to him and he supposed that he would also recover his horses; but the Kelder told him he must travel on foot and only belatedly (and after much argument) agreed to provide him with a cart. At Heidelberg he was detained for a further eighteen days in what he again describes as poor and unsatisfactory conditions until, finally, he was informed that he would not be permitted to deliver his letters and must moreover pay the costs of his detention. The decision undoubtedly pleased some of Katherine's people who had also travelled to Heidelberg, and they now approached him more civilly asking him not to report their part in the episode to the authorities in England. They returned the horses stolen at Weinheim and told his servant that they would 'provide well for his wife', but Brett was taking no chances. He announced that he would travel to Worms on leaving Heidelberg, but instead made for 'the forest towards Spyres [and] for better execution of my charge and to eschew the perils intended against me took my way towards Italy ... and arrived [safely] at Venice on Sunday, August 16th'.[16]

The Berties had seen the last of Brett and his letters, but by now there was another problem – money. It is unclear how many of the servants they had brought from England remained with them or who they had engaged since, but the cost of maintaining a family and perhaps a small retinue and moving them around Europe would have been considerable. Melissa Harkrider says that Katherine took 'many' of the exiles who joined her at Wesel into her service, and that when she relocated to Weinheim her entourage included the gentlemen John and Thomas Turpin, the merchants John Bodley and William Gosling (her one-time protector), and George Christopher, a former servant of the Marquis of Northampton, besides Bishop Barlow and others.[17] They were perhaps all economically dependent on her to some extent.

The first hint of financial difficulty is found in a letter that Myles Coverdale sent to Strasbourg, to his 'very delightful friend and brother' Conrad Hubert, Martin Bucer's former secretary, after he himself had moved to Bergzabern in the Palatinate on 20 September 1555. His language is oblique, but the emphasis on Katherine owing nothing implies that there were others who thought that she did:

With regard to the business, concerning which you requested me to enquire relating to the most illustrious Duchess of Suffolk, her very distinguished husband, whom I spoke to on this subject at Frankfort, assured me that her grace, as far as money was concerned, owed nothing at all either to our excellent father Bucer, or to any other persons. But when I shall return to Wesel, from whence I must now bring up my dear wife to this place, I will make a diligent examination into the whole business.[18]

Coverdale is quite clear that he met and spoke with Richard Bertie in Frankfurt, but what was the latter doing there and when did the conversation take place? Frankfurt is 175 miles from Wesel, so the implication is that Bertie, who now had little to do except send hopeful instructions to England, had decided to visit an old friend to relieve his boredom. Coverdale left Frankfurt for Bergzabern on 15 September, so was well placed to offer assistance when the exiles decided to abandon Wesel some months later.

Katherine had asked her cousin Francis Guevara to lend her £400 in May 1454 (before Bertie even left for the Continent),[19] and would have taken a significant sum of money to Europe with her; but as her funds dwindled she relied increasingly on what she could borrow or obtain from England. In November, shortly before she went into exile, she entrusted her lands to Walter Herenden, a religious conformist who served her as an administrator, and her Catholic mother-in-law Alice Bertie, in the hope that they would not be sequestered and she would continue to receive an income from them. A bill that would have denied refugees access to their English revenues was defeated in the Commons by William Cecil and others, but the government continued to look for ways of stemming the flow of money to Europe.[20] The Berties' access to their funds was restricted, and to make matters worse, Katherine's cousin, Lord William Willoughby of Parham (the son of her old nemesis Sir Christopher) had again claimed – just before she left England – that some of her manors were rightfully his. Fortunately she and Bertie had ensured that Herenden and their solicitor Cuthbert Brereton had access to their title deeds and other documents, and Lord William's challenge ultimately failed.[21]

Katherine and her husband could not continue to live beyond their means indefinitely – something their opponents in London would have been only too aware of – but fortunately an Evangelical minister named John a Lasco (Jan Łaski), the son of a Polish nobleman who Katherine had aided financially during his years in England, heard of their plight. A Lasco explained their situation to the King of Poland (the same Sigismund who had reportedly wanted to marry Katherine years earlier),[22] and to his brother-in-law, Nicholas 'the Red' Radziwill, the Protestant Count Palatine of Vilna (Vilnius in Lithuania), both of whom wrote to the Berties offering them what Foxe calls 'large courtesy' in their countries. 'This provision,' he says, 'unlooked for, greatly revived their heavy spirits.'[23]

The English government's attitude towards Katherine had undoubtedly hardened since she had been allowed to slip abroad virtually without hindrance, possibly because she had become a focus, a refuge, for many of the English Protestants who had chosen exile and who were now regarded as enemies of their country. More than ever, she and Bertie craved a safe, settled life for themselves and their children, but Poland was a distant country and they wanted to satisfy themselves that the offer was genuine and not merely a gesture. Perhaps it would be appropriate to let Foxe tell the next part of the story in his own words:

[Fearing that] the end of their journey should be worse than the beginning, they devised thereupon with one Master Barlow, late bishop of Chichester [*sic*],[24] that if he would vouchsafe to take some pains therein, they would make him a fellow of that journey. So, finding him prone [willing], they sent with him letters of thanks to the king and palatine; and also with a few principal jewels (which only they had left of many], to solicit for them, that the king would vouchsafe under his seal to assure them of the thing which he so honourably by letters offered.

That suit, by the forwardness of the palatine, was as soon granted as uttered; upon which assurance the said duchess and her husband, with their family, entered the journey in April 1557, from the castle of Windsheim [*sic*], where they before lay, towards Frankfort: in the which their journey, it were long here to describe what dangers fell by the way upon them and their whole company, by reason of their landgrave's captain, who, under a quarrel pretensed for a spaniel of master Berty's, set upon them in the highway with his horsemen, thrusting their boar-spears through the waggon where the children and women were, master Berty having but four horsemen with him. In the which brabble it happened the captain's horse to be slain under him.

Whereupon a rumour was sparsed [spread] immediately through towns and villages about, that the landgrave's captain should be slain by certain Walloons, which incensed the ire of the countrymen there more fiercely against master Berty, as afterward it proved. For as he was motioned by his wife to save himself by the swiftness of his horse, and to recover [reach] some town nearby for his rescue, he, so doing, was in worse case than before; for the townsmen and the captain's brother, supposing no less but that the captain had been slain, pressed so eagerly upon him, that he had [would have] been there taken and murdered among them, had not he (as God would), spying a ladder leaning to a window, by the same got up into the house, and so gone up into a garret in the top of the house, where he with his dagger and rapier defended himself for a space; but at length, the burgomaster coming thither with another magistrate which could speak Latin, he was counselled to submit himself to the order of the law. Master Berty, knowing himself clear, and the captain to be alive, was the more bold to submit himself to the judgment of the law, upon condition that the magistrate would receive him under safe-conduct, and defend him from the rage of the multitude. Which being promised, master Berty putteth himself and his weapon into the magistrate's hand, and so was committed to safe custody, while the truth of his cause should be tried.

Then Master Berty, writing his letters to the landgrave, and to the earl of Erpach, the next day early in the morning the earl of Erpach, dwelling within eight miles, came to the town wither the duchess was brought with her waggon, Master Berty also being in the same town, under custody.

The earl, who had some intelligence [knowledge] of the duchess before, after he was come and had showed such courtesy as he thought to her estate was seemly, the townsmen perceiving the earl to behave himself so humbly unto her, began to consider more of the matter; and further, understanding the captain to be alive, both they, and especially the authors of the stir, shrank away, and made all the friends they could to master Berty and his wife, not to report their doings after the worst sort. And thus master Berty and his wife, escaping that danger, proceeded in their journey toward Poland ...[25]

A tale of bold derring-do, then, but an extremely vague one. The town where the drama was played out is not identified, and the landgrave, his captain, the burgomaster and the magistrate are all nameless. We appear to be on firmer ground with the Earl of Erpach or, more usually, Erbach (Mrs Read has Erbagh), but they seem to have had no recent contact with him until this moment even though Erbach is less than thirty miles from Weinheim. A glance at the map shows that they were not very far into their journey when this incident happened, still on what might be termed 'friendly territory'; and while Foxe implies that the pet dog's behaviour was merely an excuse for the aggression he does not tell us what the real reason was. Similarly, it is not apparent how news of the incident was able to reach the town and stir up the populace before Bertie himself had time to ride there, nor is it clear what happened to the four horsemen he abandoned or how Katherine extricated herself from the melee. It is possible that

Bertie, a nearly forty-year-old administrator inclining to stoutness, really did have the makings of a D'Artagnan; but it is perhaps more likely that the story of his exploits had again grown with the telling.

Katherine was always straight-talking and not lacking in confidence, but it is surprising that even she dared to send Barlow to the king and the count to ask if their offer was to be taken seriously. Clearly, she wanted to know that she was on safe ground before embarking on a journey in excess of a thousand miles, but her request for a formal invitation under seal could – jewels or no jewels – have raised eyebrows in Poland. Fortunately, the king and the count did not take the view that their integrity was being questioned, and Barlow was able to inform his mistress that her request had (as Foxe puts it) been 'as soon granted as uttered'.

Foxe's narrative virtually ends at this point, and we can only assume that the rest their journey to Poland was largely uneventful. They reached Frankfurt without further mishap, then made their way over difficult and mountainous terrain to the plains of northern Germany from where they could turn eastwards. How they travelled and with whom, how long it took them and the places they rested, are now all lost to us, but their welcome met – and perhaps even exceeded – their expectations. Foxe says that they were 'entertained of the king, and placed honourably in the earldom of the said king of Poland, in Sanogelia [Samogitia, now in Lithuania], called Crozen, where master Berty with the duchess, having the king's absolute power of government over the said earldom, continued both in great quietness and honour, till the death of queen Mary'.[26]

The Berties cannot have reached Samogitia before July 1557 and presumably expected to remain there indefinitely; but Mary's death, on 17 November 1558, changed everything. It would have taken some time for the news to reach them, but if the story that Katherine's New Year presents to Elizabeth Tudor included 'a cushion all over richly embroidered, and set with pearls [and] the Book of Ecclesiasticus, covered with purple velvet, garnished, and clasped with silver and gilt' is accurate, it was apparently within a matter of weeks.²⁷ She was certainly aware of it when she sat down to compose a long and congratulatory letter, full of religious imagery, to the new queen on 28 January, a letter expressing her hopes for the future and eagerly anticipating her return to an unashamedly Protestant England. 'Wherefore now is our season,' she wrote, 'if any ever where, of rejoicing, and to say after Zachary, "Blessed be the Lord God of Israel," which hath visited and delivered your Majesty, and by you us, His and your miserable and afflicted subjects. For if the Israelites might rejoice in their Deborah, how much we English in our Elizabeth, that deliverance of our thralled conscience ... I greedily wait and pray to the Almighty to consummate this consolation, giving me a prosperous journey once again presently to see your Majesty, to rejoice together with my countryfolks, and to sing a song to the Lord in my native land.'²⁸

Doubtless Katherine would have preferred to leave for England immediately, but she and Bertie had assumed responsibilities in the Polish lands and could not abandon their benefactors at a moment's notice. She had apparently refrained from corresponding with William Cecil during Queen Mary's reign (presumably because she did not wish to give his rivals in the government an excuse to question his nominal conformity), but now, in February 1559, she received what was to be the first of many letters from him. Sadly, these are all lost and their content must be deduced from

Katherine's answers, but it is clear that, on this occasion, some of what she read was not to her liking. Cecil, whom Elizabeth had appointed her principal secretary, informed Katherine that while the Church in England would again become Protestant, it would not be wedded to the exiles' narrow Puritanism. Elizabeth wanted a Church that would be as inclusive as possible, a Church that retained some of the old familiar traditions; Katherine wanted one that was right-thinking – in her eyes – even if it left most people outside.

Her reply was as direct and to the point as ever. She had heard reports that Cecil was among those counselling the queen to be tolerant rather than proactive, and urged him to remember his old master the Duke of Somerset who 'being plucked of the sleeve of [by] worldly friends, for this worldly respect or that, in fine gave over [abandoned] his hot zeal to set forth God's true religion, and ... lost all that he sought to keep, with his head to boot'. She expressed admiration for Mary's commitment to the Mass – 'wherein she deserved immortal praise seeing she was so persuaded that it was good' – and urged Cecil to stand up for what he believed in even if compromise appeared to offer a quieter and more settled outcome. 'There is no fear of innovation in restoring old good law and repealing new evil,' she added, 'but it is to be feared men have so long worn the Gospel slopewise that they will not gladly have it again straight to their legs. Thus write I after my old manner, which if I persuade you, take it as thankfully and friendly as I mean it ... with my hearty prayer that God will so assist you with His grace that you may the first and only seek Him as His eldest and chosen vessel.'[29]

Cecil would not have taken offence at this – he knew Katherine too well by now – but unbeknown to her it was destined to be only the first of several disappointments. These still lay in the future, however, and in the meantime she and Bertie had to plan their return journey, a journey across Europe which would be less stressful than their earlier travels although still not without its dangers. Her four years on the run had at times taxed her endurance – and perhaps also her faith – to the uttermost, but throughout it all she had never faltered for more than a moment. Others had suffered similar tribulations, but her willingness to abandon her high social position and the risks she had taken had earned her a place in the history of her country. When Augustine Bernher dedicated a volume of Latimer's sermons to her in 1562 he referred admiringly to the 'excellent gifts of God bestowed upon your Grace, in giving unto you such a princely spirit, by whose power and virtue you were able to overcome the world, to forsake your possessions, lands and goods, your worldly friends and native country, your high estate and estimation with the which you were adorned, and to become an exile for Christ and His Gospel's sake'. He reminds her of the 'bitter morsels, which the Lord hath appointed and prepared for his chosen children and especial friends: of the which he did make you most graciously to taste, giving unto your Grace His spirit, that you were able in all the turmoils and grievances the which you did receive, not only at the hands of those which were your professed enemies, but also at the hands of them which pretended friendship and good will, but secretly wrought sorrow and mischief, to be quiet and patient, and in the end, brought your Grace home again'.[30] Interestingly, he implies that some of Katherine's troubles stemmed from failings on the part of those she had expected to help her, but does not choose to identify either the circumstances or the individuals concerned.

It could be argued that Bernher, who would have known

Katherine when he served Hugh Latimer, was in no sense a neutral or unbiased commentator, but later writers who had had little or no contact with her continued the theme. In or about 1588 one Thomas Deloney composed a ballad entitled 'The Most Rare and Excellent History of the Duchess of Suffolk and Her Husband Richard Bertie's Calamity' (to be sung to the tune of 'Queen Dido'), while in 1623 a play, *The Life of the Duchess of Suffolk* by Thomas Drew, was staged at the Fortune Theatre in Cripplegate. It may be appropriate to end this chapter with Deloney's euphoric concluding stanza:

> For when Queen Mary was deceas'd,
> The Duchess home returned again,
> Who was by sorrow quite releas'd
> By Queen Elizabeth's happy reign,
> Whose Godly life and Piety
> We May praise continually.[31]

8

LADY OF THE MANOR
1559–1565

Katherine and Richard Bertie returned to England in the late
spring or summer of 1559 and quickly re-established themselves
at Grimsthorpe. All their lands and goods were restored to them,
their debts to the Crown were cancelled, and their son Peregrine,
now almost four, was naturalised on 2 August.[1] But almost at
once there was sadness. Katherine's stepdaughter Frances had been
ailing for some time, and died, aged forty-two, on 21 November.
She was buried in St Edmund's chapel in Westminster Abbey on
5 December, and Mrs Read thought that Katherine had acted
as chief mourner: but the 'Catherine' who performed this office
was the deceased's eldest surviving daughter, Catherine Grey.[2]
The queen paid for the elaborate funeral, partly perhaps because
Frances, who was indisputably legitimate, had never pressed her
own claim to the throne.

Frances had hoped that Catherine, now nineteen, would marry
Edward Seymour, Lord Hertford, the son of the executed Duke
of Somerset, but there seemed little hope of obtaining the queen's
permission. The succession was, and would remain, uncertain,

and Elizabeth feared for the future – the future of her own unborn children – if either of the surviving Grey sisters bore a male heir. There is a tradition that the young couple asked Katherine Willoughby to intercede for them; but Katherine's influence with the queen was limited and a letter she wrote is said to have remained undelivered because Hertford lost his nerve at the last moment. The young couple married secretly in November or December 1560, and met whenever and wherever they could until Hertford went to Paris in May to complete his education. By then Catherine was pregnant, and although she concealed her condition for as long as possible she was finally left with no alternative but to confess to everything and throw herself on the queen's mercy.

Elizabeth was predictably furious. Catherine lost her place in the royal privy chamber, Hertford was recalled from France, and both were clapped into the Tower. The queen's worst fears were realised when, on 24 September, Catherine gave birth to a boy, christened Edward; and she was incandescent with rage when a second son, Thomas, arrived seventeen months later in February 1563. The Lieutenant of the Tower, Sir Edward Warner, found himself imprisoned in his own fortress for his laxity, and the young lovers were sent to separate aristocratic houses where their contact was limited to writing letters. They never saw one another again, and were not reunited until their grandson William transferred Catherine's remains from Yoxford in Suffolk (her last place of confinement) to her husband's tomb in Salisbury Cathedral at the end of the reign of James I.

Catherine was only twenty-seven when she died, probably from a combination of depression and anorexia, on 27 January 1568. Elizabeth had never forgiven her, but she was still a member of the royal family and her funeral in Yoxford church had some of the trappings of a state occasion. Her body, carefully embalmed and 'cered' (tightly wrapped in strips of cloth soaked in molten wax), was watched over by her servants until 21 February, the day of her burial, and Katherine Willoughby was probably one of the seventy-seven official mourners together with a herald and two pursuivants who represented the establishment. The deceased's arms were displayed 'everywhere' in the church, but no amount of ceremony could disguise the callousness of her treatment. Katherine had now lost two step-granddaughters, both, in the final analysis, because they stood too close to the throne.

Richard Bertie, meanwhile, settled back into the life of a country gentleman, and was elected one of two members of Parliament for Lincolnshire (William Cecil was the other), in 1563. He sat in the Commons for four years, but his record of service there was not particularly distinguished. His membership of the committee set up to consider the matter of the succession implies that the future stability of the state was high on his list of priorities, but he would have risked the wrath of a queen who did not always take kindly to suggestions that it was imperative for her to marry. In the autumn of this year Cecil suggested another way in which he could serve the Crown and England (no precise details are given), but Bertie either did not want to burden himself further or genuinely doubted his own adequacy:

As your loving commendations much comforted me, so the significations to some public function much encumbered me, yea, so much that if your gravity had not been the better known to me I should have thought it scant seriously written. But seeing you meant it faithfully, I pray you in season correct your error in preferring insufficiency for sufficiency, and to deliver yourself from rebuke and me from shame. My prayer is that I shall find you so friendly and readily hereunto inclined that I shall not need to iterate my suit.[3]

Bertie could not avoid being drawn into the orbit of the court to some extent, however, and was one of those summoned to accompany the queen when she visited Cambridge in August 1564. The royal party spent five days in the town, and he was among the courtiers honoured with the degree of Master of Arts.

Little love had been lost between Katherine and her cousin, Lord William Willoughby, but in 1564–5 the differences that had soured their relationship for nearly four decades were finally settled. It was agreed that Lord William would abandon his claim to the manors of Willoughby, Eresby, Spilsby, Toynton, Steeping and Pinchbech; while Katherine for her part would not challenge his occupation of Parham, Orford and Hogsthorpe. It is unclear why this accord could not have been reached years earlier; perhaps both parties were weary of the conflict and readier to compromise than had once been the case.[4]

Like most of her contemporaries, Katherine only really comes to our attention when something 'happens' – when, for example, she heard that fire had damaged part of the Barbican in May 1563[5] – and there must have been many days when her existence was routine, even humdrum. In the ordinary way we would know very little about this part of her life, but an account book detailing expenses incurred at Grimsthorpe in the period 1560–2 has survived and tells us a great deal about the organisation of the establishment and how money was spent.[6] It begins with a list of 'suche as dayly remayne in the housholde' headed by 'the Master [Bertie], my Lady's Grace [Katherine], Lady Elinor, Mr Peregrine and Mistress Suzan'. Lady Goff assumes that 'Lady Elinor' was

Katherine's younger stepdaughter Eleanor Clifford, but she had died in November 1547 – the identity of this Eleanor remains unknown.

Next come the servants, about a hundred in total, including a steward, a comptroller, a master of the horse, three gentlemen ushers and seven gentlemen waiters, a clerk of the provisions and a clerk of the kitchen, yeomen of the cellar and wardrobe, a butler, a pantler, yeoman ushers, footmen, a brewer, cooks, grooms of the stable and children of the kitchen, besides gardeners, dairy maids and labourers. There were also a number of 'gentlemen's servants' who presumably waited on the more senior employees, together with gentlewomen and women servants. Some of them, like the cofferer John Pretie, had shared Katherine's exile, and so too had 'Mr Coverdall, preacher', whose name appears before those of the other males listed. This was Myles Coverdale, who had also returned to England in 1559 but who had not sought or secured reappointment as Bishop of Exeter. His biographer says that he was 'penniless', and Katherine sustained him for nearly five years until he accepted the living of the church St Magnus the Martyr by London Bridge in January 1564.[7]

The average quarterly wage was 13s 4d (one mark or two-thirds of a pound), the amount paid to the master of the horse, the clerks of the kitchen and provisions, and the gentlemen ushers and waiters. Their yeoman equivalents received 10s together with the butler and the pantler; the gardeners and grooms of the stable half as much again, 15s, and the cooks and the cofferer (treasurer) 25s. Best remunerated was Myles Coverdale, who received the comparatively large sum of £5 per quarter, but his services were no doubt more highly valued than those of the others.

It is not easy to give modern (2015) equivalents for these

amounts, mainly because the problem of conversion can be approached in ways that give different and potentially widely varying answers. But the most conservative estimate is that it is necessary to multiply mid-sixteenth-century payments by a factor of at least 300, giving Coverdale (for example) an annual retainer of £6,000. This sounds comparatively modest, but we must remember that he was not required to pay council tax, did not have to worry about winter fuel bills, and was fed, and to some extent clothed, by his employer. It is worth mentioning that at the most extreme end of the scale his £20 per annum was theoretically worth £1,883,000![8]

The accounts are divided into twelve categories beginning with 'Wardrobe of Robes', the materials purchased to make clothes for Katherine and Bertie, their children, and members of the household. Richard Bertie seems to have particularly relished the access to fine clothes his new status gave him. Among the items listed are 'for bombassy [bombast, a padding for garments] for my master's satin doublet', 'ten ounces of Granado silk for my master's shirts', 'a pair of velvet shoes for my master' and 'a pair of Valencia gloves ... and a hat of thrummed silk, garnished, and a band of gold for my master at his coming to Grimsthorpe'. It is worth noting that most of these items had to be tailored on the premises – few were bought ready-made.

Less costly materials were purchased to make and decorate garments for the servants and for the ten 'children of honour', nine boys and one girl, who lived in the house and shared Suzan and Peregrine's play and lessons. These were youngsters whose parents were members of the local Lincolnshire gentry, and included John and Richard Turpin, whose older relatives had shared Katherine's exile, Richard Hall, the son of Edmund Hall, her cousin by marriage, and Anthony Blakborn, who was almost certainly related to the reliable Margaret.[9] Also mentioned are George Sebastian and George Adams, whose names sound English but who are referred to in one entry as 'the two Polish Georges'. On one occasion a lute was bought for Suzan and Peregrine, and 6s was paid for 'bowes and arrowes' for George Sebastian. This was three times as much as was spent on 'two gramer bookes'.

The next heading, 'Wardrobe of Beds', included not only the purchase of beds and coverlets but also their maintenance. The 'children of the kitchen', and presumably all the lesser servants, had to make do with straw-filled mattresses and with 'Irish rogge', a coarse frieze, for blankets; but the family and more senior officials had featherbeds with bolsters and 'white' coverlets which cost almost twenty times as much. The featherbeds were regularly 'driven', a process by which a current of air was forced through the contents to prevent them from becoming too compacted and uncomfortable to sleep on; and in November 1561 'thirteen mats to lay under beds' were purchased, although whether their purpose was to protect the beds or the sleepers from the chill of the stone floor is uncertain. Additional costs included rushes for the floors, 'a candlestick for a watche light' and 'redd lead for the stove'.

The third category, 'Gifts and Rewards', covered a multitude of expenses, not least the many sums paid to entertainers. The queen's players and trumpeters were just two of the troupes who amused the household during this period, and Katherine enjoyed the services of 'two men which played upon the puppets two nights' and of 'Mr Rose and his daughters which played before her Grace in her sickness'. Katherine contracted smallpox in the winter of 1561/2, but her illness did not prevent her from enjoying the services of performers or from playing cards. It would be interesting to know how many of those who were obliged to serve or distract her caught the virus, and how many received treatment. Were they allowed to see Doctor Keyns, whose attendance on Katherine (and also little Suzan) earned him 'a cup of silver, all gilt', or did they escape the attentions of a man whose knowledge of medicine was still founded on the ancient concepts of astrology and the internal balance of the four 'humours', blood, red choler, black choler and phlegm?

Like most members of the aristocracy, Katherine and her husband wanted to be admired for their generosity, and numerous small payments were made to local people who brought gifts of produce or performed a modest service (presumably in the hope of receiving something), and to others who had fallen on hard times. 'A poor man, one of my Lady's Grace's tenants, which found Mistress Suzan's brooch, being lost', was generously rewarded with six shillings, while 'certain women of Spilsby which bestowed wine and cakes upon Mr Peregrine and Mistress Suzan' were given 12*d* and 'a boy that gave her Grace a posy' 4*d*. Among the unfortunates was 'a poor man at the gate which had his house burnt' who was given 9*d* 'by my master's commandment', and while on a journey Katherine bestowed 20*d* on the prisoners held in Huntingdon gaol and 4*d* on 'a poor woman in the way'. 'A poor man which had been in Bedlam' got a shilling, and Suzan and Peregrine were given 2*s* 'to buy them "fayringes" of a pedlar at the gate'.

Only small sums were needed to win the goodwill of local people, but those in authority expected far more. The New Year gifts the Berties gave the queen in 1561–2 (a chess set decorated with gold and a gold necklace) cost them £30 16*s* 6*d*, and 'Mistress Ashley's man at court who let my master into the privy garden, the queen being there', was tipped 3s 4d. In February the Lord Chief Justice was presented with 'a standing cup of silver all gilt' worth £11 14s 8d, his colleague Judge Brown received one of only slightly less value, and in May a third which cost £13 7s 8d was given to the queen's attorney – Katherine and her husband may have been in dispute with the queen over the ownership of some property (discussed later), or may have been anticipating their final settlement with Lord William Willoughby. Another New Year gift went to Catherine Knollys, their Protestant friend and fellow exile, who received 'a pair of sleeves' worth £6. Peregrine and Suzan got forty shillings, double the amount they had received in 1660–1, possibly because their parents had been absent in London for the last quarter of the year.

Katherine, Bertie and (in their absence) their children were frequently invited to participate in the christenings and weddings of their servants and local people, and were expected to make an appropriate gift or bear some of the cost. When Bertie stood godfather to John Persons's child 'by his deputy' in January 1560–1 he gave 2s to the baby and 6d to the midwife; Mistress Skipwith's nurse got 5s 'when her Grace christened the child'; and 'the christening of Mr Francis Harrington's child by Mistress Suzan' cost her parents 3s 4d. Similarly, when Henry Naughton (most likely a relative of Katherine's cousin William) was married in July 1562 he was given £6 'to buy himself a gown of grogram[10] and a doublet of satin'; the vicar of Bourne, who officiated, was paid 6s, and a 'juggler with his "musisioner"' who entertained the guests afterwards got 10s.

Katherine and Bertie regularly visited other noble families in the area. In September 1562 they travelled to Launde Abbey in Leicestershire where they were entertained by Henry Cromwell, the executed Thomas's grandson, and where they tipped the servants 20s. Their next stop was at Sir Walter Mildmay's country house, Apethorpe Hall in Northamptonshire, where two keepers were given 12s and the yeomen of the wardrobe 3s 4d; and when they moved to Belvoir Castle in north-east Leicestershire the Earl of Rutland's servants got 40s and 'my Lord of Rutland's man which played upon the lute' 6s. At one point they were caught in a heavy shower, and Katherine dried herself by the fire of a wayside cottage. The householder was rewarded with a shilling.

It must be emphasised that, in most cases, these are only a few of many examples that could be given, but there were also expenses which were more probably occasional or one-offs. In March 1561–2, 6s 8d was donated 'to the collectors for Powle's steeple' – Old St Paul's Cathedral had been struck by lightning – and 'the keepers of the lions at the Tower at London' were given 6s 'by my master's commandment' the previous May. Katherine was evidently fond of birds. 'A shipman which brought her Grace a canary bird', again in March 1561–2, was rewarded with 20s, but another mariner who presented her with a parrot three months later had to be content with 3s. Monsieur Le Forge would have been gratified by the 20s he received for his gift of a book, a 'bonesetter' who reset 'two joints which were out in young Gerves's ankle' charged 3s 4d, while 'certain men which opened gaps [cleared a way] for my master and my Lady's Grace as they came from Upton' were tipped 3d. And before we leave this section, we should not forget 'Mistress Brodbank', who was paid 3s 4d 'for catching forty-four rats at Valdey' (Vaudey, a former monastic property granted to Charles Brandon and Katherine), in February 1560–1.

The fourth heading, 'Works and Buildings', covered maintenance of the Berties' properties, not least their houses at Grimsthorpe and the Barbican, and consisted mainly of payments to artificers – glaziers, slaters, carpenters and the like – and labourers. A man who laded water out of the cellar at the Barbican received 6*d*, but 'twenty women which did weed the garden and court at Grimsthorpe' got only 2*d* a day. Also mentioned here are 2*s* given to a painter 'which drew the picture of two children', and 20*d* paid to another artist 'which went to the court and drew her Grace's arms for her saddle'.

Category five, 'Husbandry', included growing crops, making farm implements, felling and cutting wood for the fires, and caring for the animals, particularly when they were ill. Some of the remedies may have been as inappropriate as those often administered to humans – in October 1560, for example, the Berties purchased 'a pound of long pepper for medicines for sick cattle'.

The sixth heading, 'Necessaries', could be taken to imply that expenses assigned to it were more essential than those in other groupings, but its real purpose was to assimilate miscellaneous outgoings that did not fit conveniently elsewhere. These included books – in January 1560–1 Myles Coverdale was reimbursed 12*s* for a copy of Eliot's dictionary and 8*s* 8*d* for four copies each of Lillie's grammars, (Plato's?) dialogues, and Aesop's fables – along with brown paper bought to 'stop cranies in the chambers' when Katherine was ill, and, more surprisingly, numerous small losses sustained gambling. Bertie, it seems, liked to bet on everything from a game of cards to which bowman would win an archery contest, and even the children were given 5*s* 'to play upon Christmas day'. The Berties were Puritans, but their brand of puritanism was concerned principally with the right interpretation of scripture and with promoting a simpler form of worship. They were not the Cromwellian killjoys of the English Civil War.

Also listed under 'Necessaries' are a number of entries which at first glance may appear puzzling. In October 1560 William King was allowed 21s 4d 'for the loss sustained by proclamation in 59 French crowns and five pistilates at the fall of gold' – a benefit also extended to several others – and the keeper of the book noted in December that 'I am to be allowed for loss sustained in £5 8s 4d Spanish money ... in four Phillips and four in dallers, 11s 6d'. The problem was devaluation. In 1542 Henry VIII, who was desperately in need of funds to fight the French, instructed the Mint to add six ounces of copper to every ten ounces of sterling silver it used to make pennies. This adulteration, which increased to as much as thirteen ounces of copper per pound in Edward VI's reign, allowed the government to spend more in the short term, but at the same time caused rampant inflation leading to widespread protests. It was left to Elizabeth to call in the debased currency and refine out the copper, but people like the Berties' servants, who had been – or who continued to be – paid with money that was not worth its face value (and this evidently included gold and silver coins from abroad), felt cheated. Katherine and her husband were sympathetic – or prudent – enough to make the deficiency good.[11]

The next five sections, 'Bakehouse and Pantry', 'Brewhouse and Buttery', 'Cellar', 'Spicery, Chaundry [where candles were kept] and Laundry' and 'Kitchen', can be conveniently taken together. The first heading included everything that was required to bake bread on the premises and 'one dozen silver plate trenchers' bought by Katherine in May 1562; the second 'four barrels of double beer and eight barrels of small beer' purchased in November 1561, followed by 'three barrels of strong beer and thirty-five of double beer' bought three months later for a total of £11 15s 4d. It is reasonable to assume that most members of the household drank it on a daily basis, and the entries under 'Cellar' indicate that the family and probably the more senior servants also consumed large quantities of wine. Claret was bought by the hogshead (a cask containing 52½ gallons), and also popular were Rhenish varieties, 'sack', dry white wines imported from southern Europe, bitter 'wormwood' and spiced hippocras.

The seasonings kept in the spicery included aniseed, cumin, pepper, ginger, cinnamon, cloves, and maces derived from nutmeg, the prices paid ranging from 8d a pound for cumin to 14s a pound for maces. 'Eight pounds and a half of wax' (for candles) cost 8s, 'a stone of candlewicks' 3s 8d and 'Mother Welcher' was paid 3d a dozen for washing thirty-three dozen 'pantry cloths' every month. The family and more senior members of the household enjoyed veal, mutton, pork, red and fallow deer, geese, woodcocks, herons and partridges, but fish was a major component of everyone's diet. 'Eight hundred salt fish' cost £26 13s 4d and 'half a hundred lings' £7 in October 1560, while in January £7 was paid for 'six barrels of white herrings' and £3 12s for 'six "cades" of red herrings'. Each 'cade' contained about 600 herrings, and quantities of other comestibles purchased were on a similar scale: 400 oranges cost 3s 10d, 420 eggs 5s 10d, and 'half a peck' of onions ('peck' used in the archaic sense of a large number) 14d. The Berties believed in stocking up out of season when prices were lower and, perhaps where heavier items were involved, the roads were more passable. Large quantities of coal for cooking purposes were purchased in April, May, June and July of 1562, and cost a total £15 18s 8d. The fires in the house itself burned wood.

Our sixteenth-century ancestors had no concept of a healthy or balanced diet, and we can only wonder how many members of the Grimsthorpe household suffered from gout, constipation or related ailments. Foods high in protein were on every menu, not least because they were more expensive and being able to afford them was a mark of gentility. Vegetables and salads that peasants grew in their gardens and apples that could be picked from trees for nothing (for example) were beneath the dignity of aristocrats like Katherine, and there is no evidence that the children were given milk to drink, again, because it was cheap and commonplace. The only fruits mentioned in the accounts are relatively costly items like figs and oranges – if there was any 'five a day' here it was five different cuts of meat!

The entries made in another, shorter book, *The booke of records for the Kychyn* for March 1561,[12] show that mealtimes at Grimsthorpe were strictly formal, with everyone being seated – and fed – according to his or her rank. The master's table was served the best fare followed by that of the gentlemen of the household, then the clerks, the yeomen and so on. The proportion of fish to meat served grew ever greater as the status of the individuals diminished, and fresh butter was reserved exclusively for the higher tables – those seated below the clerks had to make do with the salted alternative. Curiously, the family and those seated at the top table were still served two or three dishes of meat and a great variety of fish during Lent while the rest of the household made do with simpler food. They may have reduced the number of courses voluntarily, as a penance, but it could also be a case of 'do as I say, not as I do'.

The strict hierarchy of precedence that defined the household was breached only on one occasion – at Christmas, when a peasant or junior servant was created Lord (or King, Bishop or

Abbot) of Misrule for the duration of the festivities. His task was to preside over the masques, plays and feasts arranged for everyone's amusement, and he was frequently given a mock 'court' and received comic homage from the revellers. In December 1560 Katherine and Bertie gave George, Mr Pelham's man, 40s 'to furnish himself Lord of Christmas, and his men in a livery', and he subsequently received 10s as a personal gift from 'my master'. His 'furniture' cost 6s 2d.[13]

We noticed earlier that the Berties paid visits to other members of the local 'godly community', but by far their most regular journey was to London. When Katherine travelled to the capital in October 1561 she was on the road for three days and the cost of meals and accommodation for herself and her entourage amounted to £10 17s. She spent her first night at Huntingdon, having covered about forty miles from Grimsthorpe with only a stop for refreshment at Stilton in Cambridgeshire. Next day she entered Hertfordshire, pausing at Royston for dinner before moving on to Puckeridge for the night, a journey of about thirty-five miles. London was still fifty or so miles distant, but was reached late on the third day after stops for drinks at Walsworth, Ware and Hoddesdon, and dinner at Waltham Abbey. Spending many hours on poor roads either on horseback or in a conveyance without springs would have been both uncomfortable and tiring,[14] but it was essential to mix and mingle in the 'best' society and to appear both well attended and generous. Richard Bertie was accompanied by a 'train' of eighteen men and horses 'besides strangers' (costing £18 17s 1½d) when he undertook another journey in February 1560–1, and in November, Katherine paid 11s 4d 'for the suppers of twenty-four persons at the "Swan" at Charing Cross which attended upon her Grace to the court'.

The final heading, 'Stable', included food and equipment for the horses and everything necessary for their care. In October 1560 Archibald Bernard was paid £5 for a horse 'if my master likes him', and Katherine bought a 'silk fringe for a new pillion cloth' and 'a harness and trimming for the same' for 45s. 'A pair of silk reins for my Lady' set her back another 26s 8d, and two others, evidently of less quality, 'for the gentlewomen' 4s. On a more practical level, 8d was spent on 'frankincense to smoke sick horses' in October 1560, and 6s on '3 strik of dried peas' ('strik' is an old Lincolnshire word for bushel) in February 1561. The routine costs of the stable – horseshoes, saddles, straw, grain, bran, etc. – amounted to between £9 and £10 in most months.

The expenses noticed above have been categorised in the way that they appear in the account book, but this is inevitably at the expense of context. Some of the items found under different headings relate to the same moment in time, or occasion, and it may be useful to give just one example of how they can sometimes be brought together to paint a more rounded picture. Lady Goff suggests that one factor which prompted Katherine to travel to London in October 1561 was a dispute over 'some land in Lincolnshire which formerly belonged to a Mr Fulston and which was now in question between the queen and the Duchess of Suffolk'.[15] Richard Bertie was probably there already since Mistress Ashley's man had given him access to the queen's private garden in August, and it may have been Elizabeth's response – or the lack of it – that prompted him to send for Katherine. En route, she gave a total of 2s to the prisoners at Huntingdon and a poor woman she met 'in the way', and it was in November, shortly after her arrival, that she bought 'a silk fringe for a new pillion cloth' with a decorated harness and treated twenty-four attendants to supper at the 'Swan' at Charing Cross. She evidently meant to cut a figure in the streets of the capital, but before the month was out had caught smallpox – a circumstance which necessitated stuffing the cracks in her room with brown paper and employing Mr Rose and his musical daughters to help while away the hours. 'Journeying' records that hiring a 'car' 'to bring a bed from my Lady Katherine Capell's to [the] Barbican when her Grace was sick' cost 4*d* (Katherine had been staying at the court at Greenwich prior to her illness), and 'Gifts and Rewards' notes that 'Mistress Ashley's man that brought her Grace to [the] Barbican with a little wagon' (when she was clearly 'out and about' again), was paid a shilling in May 1562. She was apparently much improved by February when Dr Keynes received a silver-gilt cup for his services, and the intervening months had not been wasted. In January, the queen was given the costly New Year presents described earlier, and the Lord Chief Justice and his colleague received their 'standing cups' soon afterwards. Whether all this effort (and expense!) produced the outcome she and her husband sought is not recorded, but in March she bought a canary from a seaman and Bertie donated 6*s* 8*d* towards the repair of St Paul's steeple. Her second pet bird, a parrot, was acquired shortly before she returned to Grimsthorpe in June.

Richard Bertie did not remain in London for the whole of this period. There would have been matters in Lincolnshire that required his attention, and he was certainly there in February when 18*s* was spent on a silk hat, 'garnished and [with] a band of gold for my master at his coming to Grimsthorpe'. The frequent references to 'my master' in the accounts are added proof that although Katherine was socially superior to her husband she always deferred to him in public. When James of the kitchen was given 8*d* for 'well dressing my Lady's dinner' it was 'by my master's commandment', and the same applied to the shilling she received 'in single pence, to play at tables in her sickness'. Katherine could be dominant when she chose to be and most of the family's wealth belonged to her; but her marital arrangements were strictly conventional and entirely in keeping with her reformed faith.

It is difficult to put the Berties' expenses into context because we have no knowledge of their income and how it related to their outgoings, but there are occasional hints in the accounts that from time to time they suffered from what we would today call 'cash-flow' problems. In November Mr Bland, a skinner, was paid £14 *in part* [my italics] for furs to make Richard a gown, and a mercer, Clement Newce, got only £60 of the £178 7s 6d he was owed for 'sundry silks taken of him for my master, her Grace, the children and their servants' the following June. But there is nothing to suggest that (unlike some other aristocratic families) they were living hopelessly beyond their means, and no indication that their gambling ever threatened to ruin them. Not a little of the credit for this happy state of affairs must be given to Richard Bertie – Katherine might have married 'beneath' herself but she had chosen well.

9

A BED OF NAILS
1565–1580

By the late 1560s Katherine was approaching fifty – a good age for a Tudor lady – and doubtless hoped that her last years would be largely peaceful. But she had not reckoned with a number of events that were destined to cause her much trouble. Her first surprise came in the autumn of 1565 when she learned that her step-granddaughter Mary, the youngest of the three Grey sisters, had also contracted a secret marriage. Mary was now nineteen or twenty, small and, in the words of the Spanish ambassador, 'crook-backed and very ugly'.[1] In the course of her duties as one of the queen's maids of honour she had formed an attachment to Thomas Keyes, the sergeant porter, a widower twice her age and possibly almost twice her size. She did not dare to seek Elizabeth's permission – she had no hope of obtaining it in the aftermath of her sister Catherine's deceptions – but may have thought that marrying beneath herself would make her cousin[2] more forgiving. She wed Keyes at Whitehall on 16 July 1565 while the queen and most of the court were attending another, grander ceremony at Durham House on the Strand.

The marriage may have been secret but it was not private – one estimate puts the number of witnesses at eleven – and it was almost inevitable that it would be gossiped around the court. Whatever Mary's hopes, Elizabeth could not tolerate another act of studied disobedience, and her reaction was entirely predictable. The lovers were separated, Mary being sent to Sir William Hawtrey's recently rebuilt country house at Chequers in Buckinghamshire, while Keyes, whose position of trust as head of the palace guard made his behaviour still more shocking, was clapped into the Fleet prison. Mary was incarcerated in a room twelve feet square, maintained at minimal expense, and forbidden to meet anyone; but she cannot have suffered as much as her husband, who was kept in solitary confinement in a cell scarcely large enough to contain his huge body. Pleas for forgiveness and even an attempt to dissolve the marriage were rejected, and it may have been with some relief that Mary learned that she was to be transferred to the custody of her grandmother Katherine Willoughby. She and Hawtrey arrived at the Minories (a house near the Tower where Katherine was staying) on 7 August 1567.

Katherine was aware of her new responsibility, but the speed and the circumstances of her granddaughter's coming seem to have taken her by surprise. Mary appeared to have few of the possessions she would need to maintain herself within the household, and two days later Katherine wrote to William Cecil seeking his help:

According to the Queen's commandment, on Friday at night last, Mr Hawtrey brought my Lady Mary to the Minories to me even as I was appointed to have gone to Grimsthorpe ... The truth is, I am so unprovided of stuff here myself as at the Minories [the letter was written from Greenwich], I borrow of my Lady Eleanor and here of Mistress Sheffield; for all the stuff that I had left me when I came from the other side of the sea, and all that I have since provided for and gotten together will not sufficiently furnish our houses in Lincolnshire ... I was fain to declare the same lack of stuff to Mr Hawtrey, praying that my Lady's stuff might come before her, for the dressing up of her chamber. But would God you had seen what stuff it is! He before told me that she occupied his and none of her own [i.e. Hawtrey had himself provided for her], and now I see it I believe him well. I am sorry that I am not so well stowed for her as he was, but am compelled to borrow it from my friends in the town. She had nothing but an old livery feather bed, all too torn and full of patches, without either bolster or counterpane, but two old pillows, the one longer that the other, an old quilt of silk so torn as the cotton of it comes out, such a little piteous canopy of red sarcenet [fine thin silk] as were scant good enough to hang over some secret stool [toilet], and two little pieces of old, old hangings, both of them not seven yards broad. Wherefore I pray you heartily consider of this, and if you shall think it meet, be a mean for her to the Queen's Majesty that she might have the furniture of one chamber for herself and her maid, and she and I will play the good housewives and make shift with her old bed for her man.³ Also, I would if I durst beg further some old silver pots to fetch her drink in, and two little cups ... one for beer another for wine. A basin and a ewer [for washing] I fear were too much, but all these things she lacks and were meet she had, and hath nothing in this world. And truly, if I were able to give it her, she should never trouble her Majesty for it; but look ye, what it shall please her Majesty to appoint for her shall be always ready to be delivered in as good case as by her wearing of it, it shall be left, whensoever it shall please her Majesty to call for it. I hope she will do well hereafter, for notwithstanding that I am sure she is now glad to be with me, yet I assure you she is otherwise, not only in conscience but in very deed, so sad and ashamed of her fault (I think it is because she saw me not since before) so that I am not yet sure she can get her to eat, in all that she hath eaten now these two days not so much as a chicken's leg. She makes me even afraid of [for] her, and therefore I will be the gladder for them [the items requested]. I think a little comfort would do well.[4]

If readers feel they have been here before they should turn back some twenty years and five chapters to the time when Katherine was asked to look after little Mary Seymour. Her protests then sound strangely familiar, and both are examples of her reluctance to contribute to the maintenance of someone who (in her eyes) was not her responsibility. She may indeed have had to refurbish her houses after her return from exile, but she was surely not so ill-provided seven years later that she could not find Mary Grey a decent bed and a few pots. Again, the burden was unwelcome and she was nobody's fool.

Mary remained with Katherine for almost two years until she was moved to the London home of the rich merchant Sir Thomas Gresham in June 1569. Not much is known of this phase of her life, but she was further saddened by the deaths of her sister Catherine (in January 1568) and her husband Thomas Keyes, in late August or the beginning of September 1571. Keyes had been released from the Fleet a year earlier and given a post at Sandgate Castle in Kent; but his tentative request to be permitted to live with his wife was rejected and they never saw each other again. It was perhaps small consolation that Elizabeth could now take the view that whatever threat Mary posed to her had been lifted, and could accede to Gresham's request to discharge her in May 1572. After spending some months with her stepfather Adrian Stokes at Beaumanor in Leicestershire she secured a house of her own in London, and her income increased as she was gradually restored to royal favour. She was again appointed a maid of honour to the queen at the end of 1577,[5] but died, possibly from plague, on 20 April the next year. In her will she left her mother's gold bracelets and a 'mystic ruby', thought to have magical properties, to 'her very good lady and grandmother' Katherine Willoughby, with the request that Katherine give something to Suzan. Suzan was the chief mourner at her funeral, held in Westminster Abbey on 14 May.

Suzan was by this time in her mid-twenties, and in late 1570 or early 1571 had married Reginald Grey, heir to the earldom of Kent. Given her mother's strong views on the subject, we may assume that Reginald was Suzan's own choice, but his situation was far from satisfactory. His half-uncle, Richard, Earl of Kent, had gambled away so much of the family fortune that Henry, his father, lacked the wherewithal to claim the title, and Katherine felt she must do everything she could to help him recover it. At the same time she hoped the queen would confer her barony of Willoughby d'Eresby on her husband Richard, notwithstanding his relatively humble origins, and asked William Cecil to again be her friend.

Her first letter on the subject to Cecil is dated 29 July 1570, and was written from Wrest, the Greys' house in Bedfordshire, 'bleared', as she terms it, by a 'grieved heart' and a 'shaking hand'. In it, she asks him to hand her request to Elizabeth personally but discreetly, so as not to alert potential opponents. She vouchsafes that Richard Bertie will give his son-in-law land worth £100 as a dowry, and trusts that Cecil will 'find both honour and comfort in helping such a one as will be ever ready to do what in him lies to deserve his [Cecil's] courtesy and to account him patron of all his good hopes'.[6] Five days later she thanks him for his answer 'with his good furtherance of the same, praying him, as occasion shall serve, to help perfect what is well begun'. She has been cheered by his apparent expectation that her son-in-law to be would be granted the earldom – 'of Mr Grey you speak somewhat comfortably' – but expresses concern that there had been little or no mention of Bertie's barony. The main thing, she implies, is that there are some positive developments before she has to face the guests at Suzan's wedding.[7]

Richard Bertie would doubtless have liked to become Lord Willoughby, to be 'upwardly mobile', but knew he would encounter opposition in what was still a markedly conservative and hierarchical society. In a letter to Cecil written at the beginning of September he complains that the Earl of Arundel 'told the queen I was no gentleman … [but] I am no wit ashamed of my parents, being free English, neither villains nor traitors. And if I would, after the manner of the world bring forth old abbey scrolls for matter of record, I am sure I can reach back as far backward as Fitzalan [Arundel]'. He admits that he is 'not a gentleman of the first escutcheon', but emphasises that his father's right to bear arms was confirmed by the heralds in Henry VIII's time.[8]

Cecil urged Katherine to raise these matters with the queen herself 'when her Majesty comes near', but this only threw her into a greater quandary. Elizabeth was then at Penley, only about twelve miles from Wrest, but Katherine had heard that she was shortly to depart for Kenilworth and asked her friend to advise precisely when and where it would be best to approach her. If he thought sooner was better than later, could he, she asked, arrange for the royal harbingers to provide her with accommodation about the court at Penley, because it would not be possible for her 'to go home the same night'.[9]

Unfortunately, we again lack Cecil's side of the correspondence and so cannot say exactly what happened next or when; but there is evidence that both he and Elizabeth began to find Katherine's constant importuning tiresome. There were more letters and a face-to-face discussion with the queen in April and May 1571, but the omens were no longer propitious. Cecil had apparently given her short shrift on one occasion – Katherine blamed his gout when he made 'such haste' from her – and she was troubled by 'Her Majesty's strange countenance and your Lordship's short words'.[10] After meeting the queen again she wanted to tell him what had passed between them, 'but seeking you in your chamber I could not find you'.[11] Even old friendships can be strained sometimes, and one cannot help wondering if this was an occasion when Cecil made himself scarce!

The fact of the matter is that although there were few things more important to Katherine than her husband and her son-in-law, Cecil and his royal mistress had far more to worry them than two questionable claims to peerages. In May 1568 Mary, Queen of Scots escaped from Lochleven Castle and came south hoping that her 'good sister' Elizabeth would help her recover her kingdom. She found, however, that she had only exchanged one prison for another, and her continued detention in England made her a focus of opposition for the next nineteen years. In the winter of 1569 the Catholic earls of Northumberland and Westmoreland rose in a short-lived revolt 'for the reformation of religion and preservation of the person of the Queen of Scots',[12] a rebellion that served to remind Elizabeth that not all her subjects were devoted to her. The situation became still more acute in February 1570 when Pope Pius

V formally declared her deposed and absolved English Catholics of their allegiance, a decision that allowed opponents at home and abroad to conspire against her without searching their consciences or endangering their immortal souls.

These matters concerned Cecil as much – if not more – than they concerned Elizabeth, but at least the queen was not burdened with the multiplicity of relatively minor problems that crossed Cecil's desk every working day. Tudor ministers, as M. A. R. Graves points out, were also bureaucrats; no protocols defined what matters a Secretary of State should, or should not, deal with, and Cecil found himself attending to 'high policy' in one moment and to 'pettifogging detail' in the next.[13] During part of the period under consideration (i.e. 1567–9) we find him dealing with letters from a Mr Waad expressing the view that Piers Edgcombe was a fit man to be knighted, from James Spencer who wrote from Danzig 'concerning forces raising for the Prince of Orange and for the King of Denmark', and from the Archbishop of Canterbury recommending a scheme to make the river to Canterbury navigable. A Mr Stene asked that he might not in his old age be discharged from his rectory of Higham, John Lauson wrote to him 'concerning Laurence Thornton's committing a burglary upon his brother', and the redoubtable John Foxe petitioned that 'a law for printing that allows not of above four strangers in one place' be dispensed with so that his martyrology 'might be soonest printed'. Peter Osborne asked that trade with Portugal should be 'free and open', Bernard Randolph, the Common Sergeant of London, wrote about 'a person who was apprehended for stealing brass and copper from the tomb of Henry VII', and the Bishop of London sought his aid in obtaining dowries for his three orphaned nieces. One correspondent, John Gordon, wrote to him in six languages

(Syriac, Ethiopic, Arabic, Hebrew, Greek and Latin) 'owning his relieving him when destitute and begging some employment' – it is perhaps hardly surprising that the Bishop of Ely compared him to Moses and Joseph when he congratulated him on his 'good management of the public affairs'.[14]

In the end Katherine's petitions were partially successful. Reginald Grey did indeed become Earl of Kent for a short period (he died in March 1573), but there was to be no barony for Richard Bertie. Bertie sent Cecil a collection of court rolls and other papers relating to his claim in April 1572. The Attorney General, Sir Gilbert Gerrard, and the Solicitor General, Thomas Bromley, gave their opinions, and he was led to believe that Elizabeth would soon reach a decision. But nothing happened, and he had to accept that, in his case, his wife's wishes would not be granted. Prejudice and snobbishness were certainly to blame in some measure, but another factor was the possibility that he might outlive Katherine, perhaps by many years. As matters stood, Peregrine would become Lord Willoughby on the death of his mother, but if Bertie were to be ennobled he would have to wait for his father to die too.

Unsurprisingly perhaps, Bertie corresponded with Cecil on other matters that affected both his and his wife's interests. In September 1568 he proffered his thanks for previous favours, and when, three years later, he heard that the queen was about to grant a lease of customs, begged Cecil to use his influence to ensure that their rights in the port of Boston were not affected.[15] In 1569 he took time to remind their good friend of the suit of a poor Dutchman who was anxious to return to Holland to collect his wife and goods; and the following June he sought his backing for efforts he was making to settle 'stranger [foreign] artificers' in Stamford. He also spent long hours writing a rebuttal to Knox's *First Blast of the Trumpet Against the Monstrous Regiment of Women*, which, as we have seen, raised strong objections to female authority. As a staunch Protestant himself, Bertie might have been expected to share Knox's opinions, but in some areas both he and Katherine seem to have been considerably in advance of their times.[16]

Peregrine Bertie was not particularly like his father, nor, for that matter, like Katherine's other sons. When he grew older he would make his reputation as a soldier rather than as a scholar or administrator, and he did not, apparently, display the meek obedience of his two half-brothers. In his youth he was sent to reside in William Cecil's household, 'boarded out' after the custom of the era, but word reached his mother that his behaviour there was not always satisfactory. On one occasion she asked Cecil 'to give that young man my son some good counsel, to bridle his youth, and with all haste to dispatch him the court, that he may go down to his father while I trust all is well'.[17] Perhaps he was more wilful, more determined to enjoy life, than her other children, and she found it hard to accept that her only surviving son was not as 'perfect' as she would have wished.

Peregrine's choice of a wife also caused his mother much heartache. When he was about seventeen, he was linked with Elizabeth Cavendish, daughter of the infamous Bess of Hardwick; but nothing came of the proposal and in 1578 he wed the Earl of Oxford's sister, Mary de Vere. Oxford was unhappily married to Ann, William Cecil's daughter, and Katherine appears not to have liked either him or Mary; but such was her aversion to 'arranged' or enforced unions that her opposition was limited to unburdening herself on Cecil and confronting Mary with her usual forthrightness. On 2 July 1577 she told her friend,

It is very true that my wise son has gone very far with my Lady Mary Vere: I fear too far to turn. I must say to you in counsel what I have said to her plainly, that I had rather he had matched in any other place, and I told her the causes. Her friends made small account of me. Her brother did in him lay to 'defase' my husband and my son. Besides our religions agreed not, and I cannot tell what more. If she should prove like her brother, if an empire followed her [i.e. even if she were one of the greatest ladies in Christendom] I should be sorry to match so. She said that she could not rule her brother's tongue, nor help the rest of his faults: but for herself she trusted so to 'use' her as I should have no cause to mislike of her; and seeing it was so far forth between my son and her, she desired my good will, and asked no more. That is a seemly thing, quoth I, for you to live on; for I fear that Mr Bartrey [Bertie] will so mislike of these dealings, that he will give little more than his good will if he give that. Besides if her Majesty shall mislike of it, sure we turn him to the wild world. She told me how Lord Sussex and Mr Hatton had promised to speak for her to the Queen, and that I would require you to do the like. I told her her brother used you and your daughter so 'elve' [evil] that I could not require you to deal in it. Well, if I would write, she knew you would do it for my sake; and since there was no undoing it she trusted I would for my son's sake help now. [several sentences mutilated] ... and therefore kept him from the Court till her Majesty found fault with me and said I did it 'in a stomach' against her; but God knows I did it not so, but for fear of this marriage and quarrels. Within this fortnight there was one spoke to [me] for one Mistress Gaymege, an heir of [a] thousand marks land, which had been a meeter [better] match for my son.[18]

Lady Mary had clearly tried to distance herself from her brother in the hope of winning Katherine over, but the outcome would depend ultimately on whether their respective friends could persuade the queen to give her consent to the match or withhold it. Katherine implied that she was reluctant to ask Cecil to become involved in the matter, but only twelve days later wrote to him again from Willoughby House (as she now termed the Barbican) enclosing a letter from her husband expressing his reservations. Bertie was (presumably) at Grimsthorpe, and Katherine made it clear that she had not told him the full story 'because if he knew as much as I of Lord Oxford's dealings, it would trouble him more; but the case standing as it doth, I mean to keep it from him'. She adds, sorrowfully, 'I cannot express how much it grieveth me that my son in this weightiest matter hath so forgotten himself to the trouble and disquiet of his friends.'[19]

Unfortunately for Peregrine, Oxford disliked the Berties as much as they loathed him, and he soon realised that the earl would not welcome him as a prospective brother-in-law. This and the uncertainty over whether the queen would, or would not agree to the union caused him considerable anguish, a disquiet that punctuates almost every line of a letter he wrote to Mary in the autumn of 1577:

My own good Lady, I am not little grieved that I have not or this time resolved the doubt I left you in, and so much the more as I fear it hath caused your unquietness, in whom I make more account of than of myself or life, and therefore, resolve yourself that if I had had fit time, I would not [have] so slightly overpassed it. But the truth is, by other troubles, I have yet heard nothing of that matter worth the sending, yet, did I think not to lose so much occasion, since I know not when to recover it again, as to let [you] understand how uncourteously I am dealt with by my Lord, your brother, who, as I hear, *bandeth* against me, & sweareth my death, which I fear nor force not, but lest his displeasure should withdraw your affection towards me, otherwise I think no way to be so offended as I can not defend. And thus good Lady persuade yourself no less than you shall find I will give cause or perform. Above all things if you wish me well let nothing grieve you whatsoever you shall hear do hap. For my own part my good or evil fortune consisteth only in you, whom I must request to accept as well this scribbled well meaning as better eloquence, excusing my imperfections with my troubled mind, which am locked up so fast as I could scarce get pen & paper to be the present messengers of my poor good will, and thus end a wilful man, having received new occasion by your letter at this instant to trouble you more hereafter withal. From Willoughby House. Yours more than his own and so till his end. Peregrine Bertie.[20]

He need not have worried. The queen gave her consent, probably soon after Christmas, and Oxford and the Berties were obliged to accept her decision. In July, Katherine had told Cecil that 'if her Majesty could be won to like of it, my husband would be the easier won to it, if Lord Oxford's great uncourtesy do not too much trouble him',[21] and she herself decided that it would be better to make a friend of Mary when it seemed there was no going back. By December they were conspiring to effect a reconciliation between Oxford and his estranged wife by tricking the earl into showing affection for his infant daughter whom he had hitherto refused to see. Katherine informed Cecil that

on Thursday I went to see my Lady Mary Vere. After other talks, she asked me what I would say to it if my Lord her brother would take his wife again. 'Truly,' quoth I, 'nothing would comfort me more, for now I wish to your brother as much good as to my own son.' 'Indeed,' quoth she, 'he would very fain see the child and is loth to send for her.' 'Then,' quoth I, 'and you will keep my counsel, we will have some sport with him. I will see if I can get the child hither to me, when you shall come hither, and whilst my Lord your brother is with you I will bring in the child as though it were some other of my friends' and we shall see how nature will work in him to like it, and tell him it is his own after.' 'Very well,' quoth she, 'we agree thereon.' ... I mean not to delay in it otherwise than it shall seem good to your Lordship and in that sort that may best like you. I will do what I can either in that or in anything else that may any way lay in me.[22]

Later that day Katherine thoughtfully wrote to Cecil's wife Mildred, who had been caring for the child, apologising for seeking to deprive her of her granddaughter, but there is no evidence that the ruse was ever attempted. Perhaps Cecil advised against it? In any event, the Oxfords were reconciled, although not until several years later.

After Peregrine and Mary were married they set up home at Grimsthorpe while Katherine and Bertie took a house in Hampstead away from the bustle of central London. The newly-weds should have been more than content with their situation after so many uncertainties, but instead began to drink heavily and neglect the property. Their behaviour alarmed Katherine, and once again it was Cecil who had to listen to her troubles poured out in a letter dated 12 March 1578. 'My daughter[-in-law] Mary and her husband,' she complains, 'will in any wise use a house out of hand, and I fear will so govern it as my husband and I shall have small comfort of it and less gain; for what disorders they make we must pay for it, but neither the young folk nor my husband so considers of it yet.' She admits that 'my Lady [Mary] loves wine who knows her that knows not that ... and my son hates it not'; but still asks Cecil to send them two tuns of the stuff, perhaps, as Mrs Read suggests, to keep them at Grimsthorpe rather than have them turn up in the capital – 'if they outrage not too much so as we shall not be able to bide it'.[23]

The situation was apparently no better by September when Thomas Cecil, William's eldest son, proposed to call at Grimsthorpe in the course of what he calls 'a little progress into Lincolnshire'. He tells his father that he will have better knowledge of 'such disagreements as have fallen out there' after his visit, but that he understands 'that my Lady of Suffolk's coming down from London was to appease certain unkindness grown between her son and his wife'.[24] Peregrine and Mary were clearly not 'getting on' well together, but the well-meaning mother-in-law's intervention only served to alienate Mary and led to the situation described in the Prologue. On Easter Monday 1580 Katherine wrote what was to be her last letter to Cecil (the last one that has been preserved), asking him to use his influence to persuade the authorities to allow her son to go abroad:

> I am ashamed to be so troublesome to your Lordship and others of my good Lords of her Majesty's honourable council, specially in so uncomfortable a suit as for licence of their assent of the absence of my only dear son, in whose company I hoped with comfort to have finished my last days. But ... either I must see his doleful pining and vexed mind at home, which hath brought him to such a state of mind and body as so many knoweth and can witness it, or else

content myself with his desire to seek such fortune abroad as may make him forget some griefs and give him better knowledge and experience to serve her Majesty and his country at his return. The time he desireth for the same is five years, so I am never like after his departure to see him again; yet am I loath he should so long be out of her Majesty's realm wherefore I cannot consent to any more than three years. Oh, my good Lord, you have children and therefore you know how dear they be to their parents, your wisdom also is some help to govern your fatherly affections by ... but alas, I a poor woman which with great pains and travail many years hath by God's mercy brought an only son from tender youth to man's state ... so hoping now to have reaped some comfort for my long pains ... in place of comfort I myself must be the suitor for his absence, to my great grief and sorrow. But God's will be fulfilled, who worketh all for the best to them that love and fear Him; wherefore were not that hope of Him thoroughly settled in me, I think my very heart would burst for sorrow. I understand my sharp letters be everywhere showed, but were the bitter causes that moved them as well opened and known, I am sure my very enemies ... would not only pity me and my husband's wrongs but both my children's ... I most humbly beseech her Majesty even for God's sake therefore to give him leave to go to sea and live in all places where it shall please God to hold him, always with the duty of a faithful subject to serve ... her Majesty ...[25]

In the event Peregrine did not go abroad until two years after his mother's death, and her fears for him proved groundless. His marital difficulties were resolved – he and Lady Mary produced five sons and a daughter – and his skill in the art of warfare earned him not only fame but the gratitude of his queen.

It would, however, be wrong to give the impression that Katherine spent much of the 1570s fretting about her husband, her son, and her son-in-law. On the contrary, she remained dedicated to her interpretation of religion, and few things mattered more to her than persuading her tenants and members of the wider Lincolnshire community to see things her way. England was now once more a Protestant country, but in many local parishes congregations sought to keep their altars and rituals while the clergy continued to dress after the old manner. Katherine had no time for the veneration of saints' images or the wearing of surplices (to name just two practices she would have associated with Catholicism), but the queen, as we have already noticed, was more tolerant. The Elizabethan religious settlement had embraced some of the old customs within a Protestant framework, and seeking further reform – exceeding the official line on such matters – risked bringing the reformers into conflict with the state.

In the years after her return from exile, Katherine re-established her 'godly household' at her principal residences in Lincolnshire and London, appointed reformers as her chaplains, employed itinerant Protestant ministers as preachers, and bought Bibles and other devotional literature for her dependants. On two occasions she interceded for her spiritual mentor John Browne when the Council obliged him to defend his criticisms of the established church in the Star Chamber, and gave financial help to others who shared her opinions. Her main task, however, was to bring those who were in error (as she saw it) to a 'right' understanding of the gospel, and it was to this end that she reached beyond her homes and her circle into the wider community. She held, or presented clergy to, no fewer than twenty-two benefices in Lincolnshire in the course of her lifetime, and used her influence to advance suitably 'godly' incumbents and promote Protestantism through education. The fact that eight of the nine clerics whose marital status is known were married is itself proof of their detachment from the old faith; and it is no coincidence that with one exception they all resided in their parishes. It helped to ensure that the message was rammed home.[26]

Katherine was not greatly troubled by illness in the earlier part of her life – she is reported as suffering from ague (alternate sweating and shivering) in 1537 and we have already noticed her brush with smallpox over the winter of 1561/2 – but she was increasingly troubled by health issues as she grew older. She was very sick in the late summer of 1568 when Richard Bertie referred in a letter to Cecil to 'the rumour of the duchess's dangerous illness spreading over the land [that] could not be hid from the court'; but by the time he wrote he was able to pass on the information that 'my Lady, though she continue a bedwoman, and not a footwoman, yet, God be praised, she groweth a little stronger than her sickness, and sendeth to you, and to my lady, your wife, as strong and hearty commendations as ever she did'.[27] We do not know what this ailment was or whether Katherine ever fully recovered from it, but in August 1570, when she was at Wrest trying to secure the earldom of Kent for her future son-in-law, Bertie apparently had to be sent for, although on his arrival he found her 'somewhat eased of her extreme fits'.[28] When Cecil inquired after her health the following April she told him she 'was yet not very well, for that I took upon me a greater journey that I was well able to endeavour after my long sickness'.[29]

Katherine still had another nine years to live at this point, but could have feared it would be much less at this moment. She was apparently reasonably well in 1577 if her attempts to influence her son's marriage and improve the relationship between Cecil's daughter and the Earl of Oxford are anything to go by, but the deterioration in her health became more marked thereafter. By September 1579 she was so unwell that one of her footmen apparently hinted to Cecil that she was losing her grip, a suggestion which upset her and which she rebuffed in the strongest terms:

> I beseech you my good Lord not to think, though I be sickly that I am altogether senseless as my foolish footman hath given your Lordship rather to think. I assure you, since yesternight that my daughter came from London and told it me, I have not been quiet, as this bearer can tell whom I have dispatched so soon as my extremity would suffer me to write this letter. And where it pleaseth you of your goodness to consider of any by his foolish talk ... I beseech your Lordship for God's sake there may be no more words of it ... Craving your pardon both for my foolish man and myself ... at Hampstead, in pain of body as this bearer can tell.[30]

Katherine still retained all her old feistiness, but the end was now approaching. She died a year later, on 19 September 1580, although whether at Grimsthorpe or in London is not known.

Postscript

THE RAVAGES OF TIME

Katherine's death would have saddened not only her husband and children but also her servants, who had found her a fair-minded mistress, and those in the wider Protestant community who knew her as a loyal and committed friend. Richard Bertie must have received many expressions of condolence, but only one survives among the family papers. This was written by Johan Landshade de Steinach from Turlaco (Spain) on 24 November 1580, and praises Katherine's piety and virtues, particularly the fortitude with which she bore her exile, before reflecting on the undoubted happiness of her present state. He goes on to express his gratitude towards her for maintaining his son in her household for the past three years, and says that he would willingly leave him in Bertie's care; but because the boy's mother is anxious to see him he has 'yielded to her pleadings' and asked Mr Bartholomew Hylles 'to send him back by some merchant coming to the next Frankfurt fair'.[1]

Katherine's elegantly arranged funeral took place at Spilsby on Saturday 22 October 1580. The chief mourner was her daughter Suzan, and the ten women who accompanied her included four titled ladies, 'the Lady Zouche widow, the Lady Willoughby of Parham, the Lady "Sicill" and the Lady Wrey'. Margaret, Lady Willoughby of Parham, was her cousin by marriage, Lady 'Sicill' was presumably Mildred Cecil, who should more properly have been styled Lady Burghley, and Anne, Lady Wrey (Wray), was the wife of Sir Christopher Wray of Glentworth (Lincolnshire), judge and sometime speaker of the House of Commons. The identity of Lady Zouche is less certain because the widows of the eighth and tenth Lords Zouche of Harringworth were still living in 1469 and we have no date of death for either of them or for the widow of the ninth lord. The tenth lord's widow, Mary or Margaret Welby, came from Moulton in Lincolnshire, about twenty miles from Grimsthorpe, so perhaps she is the most likely candidate of the three.[2]

These ladies were escorted by two 'assistants to the chief mourner' (Peregrine, now Lord Willoughby de Eresby, and William, Lord Willoughby of Parham), the preacher, the Dean of Lincoln, and the great banner bearer, Sir William Skipwith. Then came the four 'bearers of the bannerolles', the four bearers of the corpse, the four assistants to the bearers, the two 'officers' and the two gentlemen ushers. Only men were allowed to occupy these positions, and those chosen included long-standing associates like Edmund Hall and Francis Guevara, who have already featured in our story, together with four members of the Jenny family, Ralph Chamberlain, George Metham and William Fitzwilliam. The Jennys were distant relatives, Chamberlain a Catholic gentleman who had been on good terms with Katherine, Metham had served as standard bearer at Charles Brandon's funeral, and Fitzwilliam was presumably the sometime Lord Deputy of Ireland who was a cousin of Mildred Cecil. Most were provided with mourning garments – gowns with hoods made from different lengths of material according to rank – and the peers and peeresses received apparel for their servants as well.

The manner of proceeding to the church and the order in which the mourners made their offerings were also governed by strict precedence. 'Poor men, poor women, singing men and chaplains' led the procession followed by the invited mourners, Garter king of arms and Somerset herald, and lastly, 'the body with assistants under a canopy' and 'the chief mourner between two lords'. This was reversed for the offering, where Suzan offered first and the others after her. Unfortunately, our narrative ends at this point, but when the solemnities concluded the guests would have been liberally entertained and the poor who had attended given some money.[3]

One person who – surprisingly, to our way of thinking – was not present on this occasion was the grieving widower Richard Bertie. The reason was that it was not then customary for husbands to attend their late wives' funerals, possibly because the deceased's closest female relative always acted as chief mourner. This was one occasion when a younger brother did not automatically take precedence over an older sister – Suzan was pre-eminent at her mother's obsequies although her brother Peregrine, the heir to the title, was also present, and readers may recall that it was Frances, and not *her* brother the young Earl of Lincoln, who had fulfilled the role at their mother Mary Brandon's funeral. Charles Brandon, her widower, likewise had no part to play.[4]

Katherine's finest memorial is her monument in the Willoughby chapel at Spilsby. Like the rest of the effigies in the chapel, it is in a remarkably good state of preservation, and has fortunately avoided the attentions of puritan iconoclasts. It is somewhat curious that

Katherine and Bertie should have sought to preserve their memory in stone after the manner of their Catholic ancestors, and stranger still to find that five of the six texts on the western-facing side of the structure are written in Latin. This sits oddly with their desire to make the Bible widely available in translation, and could imply that even they found some of the old customs hard to abandon. To the south is an image of Peregrine standing in an arched niche above a semi-reclining effigy of his only daughter, Catherine, who died in childbed in 1610.

A church enjoys a permanence not always extended to more secular buildings, and several of Katherine's dwelling houses have all but disappeared. Suffolk Place in Southwark, where Charles Brandon entertained Henry VIII and the Emperor Charles V in 1522, was demolished forty years later, and Willoughby House exists only in a name given to part of the modern Barbican development in Cripplegate. The same is true of Westhorpe House in Suffolk. In *The Historic Sites of Suffolk*, published in 1839, John Wodderspoon recorded that 'the workmen are now pulling it down, as fast as may be, in a very careless and injudicious manner. The coping bricks, battlements, and many other ornamental pieces are made of earth, and burnt hard, and as fresh as when first built. They might, with care, have been taken down whole, but all the fine chimneys and ornaments were pulled down with ropes, and crushed to pieces, in a most shameful manner. There was a monstrous figure of Hercules, sitting cross-legged with his club, and a lion beside him, but all shattered to pieces.'[5] No image survives, but many pieces of debris recovered from the moat in the 1990s bear traces of finely carved reliefs.

Fortunately, three of the other properties Katherine occupied at various times, Parham, Tattershall and Grimsthorpe, have fared rather better. Parham (now Moat) Hall, where she was born, is described by Pevsner as a 'wonderful survival ... a moated early sixteenth-century timber-framed house with substantial brick parts'. There are two- and three-light windows with arched lights, 'rather low on the ground floor, tall and with transom on the first floor', and a fine gable to the west. The gateway has a four-centred arch and two niches with wild men, heraldic symbols of the Willoughby family's Ufford ancestors.[6]

The first castle at Tattershall was begun by Robert de Tateshale in 1231, but it was Ralph, Lord Cromwell, Henry VI's treasurer, who built the great tower and constructed a second outer moat to embrace three new ranges of service buildings between 1432 and 1448. Cromwell's design was intended more to create an impression than to withstand a siege, and the complex dominated the surrounding countryside when the king granted it to Charles Brandon in 1537. It was subsequently owned and occupied by the earls of Lincoln, but became derelict and ruinous around 1700. Over the years many of the outer buildings were demolished, the moats were filled in, and even the four great fireplaces were no longer in situ when Lord Curzon acquired the site in 1911. His intervention frustrated a plan to demolish the tower brick by brick and ship it to America, and he arranged for the return of the fireplaces while securing the remainder of the structure and the other surviving buildings. The property has been in the care of the National Trust since 1925.

Brandon's greatest building project was at Katherine's house at Grimsthorpe in Lincolnshire which became their permanent country residence in the aftermath of the Lincolnshire rebellion. This time he used stone – easily obtained from the nearby redundant abbey of Vaudey – and constructed the basic form of the house we still see today. The north front was redesigned by Sir John Vanburgh at the beginning of the eighteenth century and a new Tudor-style west front was erected after 1811, but much of Brandon's work remains in the south and east ranges. Inside, the great hall, with its full-length figures of monarchs who favoured the family, is perhaps Vanburgh's greatest achievement, but other parts of the house retain something of their Tudor ambience. It is still occupied by the present Lady Willoughby de Eresby.[7]

Reminders of Katherine are not, however, confined only to bricks and mortar. The forty-four letters she wrote to William Cecil (listed in Appendix 1), reveal her personality in a way that no building project or biographer writing for a patron could ever do, and despite all their infelicities are still arguably her finest memorial. A glance at the list is enough to show that there were occasions when two or three letters were written in quick succession, but that there are also 'gaps' in the correspondence of several years duration. It is highly improbable that Katherine sometimes failed to write to Cecil for years on end (except, perhaps during Queen Mary's reign when she was in exile), and the only logical conclusion is that, in common with Cecil's others papers, much has survived but much has also been lost. Katherine must have written many letters to others, family members and private individuals, that have long since vanished, but enough remains to inform us that here was a single-minded woman of unshakable conviction. 'A woman,' as Lady Goff called her, 'of the Tudor Age.'

Appendix 1

KATHERINE WILLOUGHBY'S CORRESPONDENCE WITH WILLIAM CECIL

These are listed in the following:

Calendar of State Papers Domestic Series, Edward VI 1547–1553, ed. C. S. Knighton (revised edn, 1992). 'CSP 1'

Calendar of State Papers Domestic Series, Edward VI, Mary, Elizabeth, 1547–1580, ed. R. Lemon (1856). 'CSP 2'

Historical Manuscripts Commission, *Calendar of the Manuscripts of the Marquis of Salisbury preserved at Hatfield House, Hertfordshire*, Part 1 (1883), Part 2 (1888) & Part 13 (1915). 'Salisbury'

A Catalogue of the Lansdowne Manuscripts in the British Museum (British Museum Department of Manuscripts, 1819, reprinted 2012). 'Lansdowne'

In Edward VI's reign:

1. 1548 (no day or month). 'Concerning the Queen's child [Mary Seymour] lodged at her house, with an account of plate belonging to the nursery.' Lansdowne, Num. 2, 17, pp. 7–8. Followed by 'A

letter of the Duke of Somerset to Wm. Cecil, Esq., to deliver some writing to the Duchess of Suffolk'. Lansdowne, Num. 2, 18, p. 8.

2. 24 July 1549. Protests the expense of maintaining 'the late queen's child'. CSP 1, no. 332, pp. 127–8.

3. 11 November 1549. 'Declaring her concern for Cecil, on some troubles he was now in, being discharged of his place in the D. of Somerset's family; probably of Master of Requests'. Lansdowne, Num. 2, 24, p. 8.

4. 28 December 1549. Enigmatic. CSP 1, no. 429, p. 158.

5. 25 March 1550. Expresses her concern for the imprisoned Duke of Somerset, and wonders how she can best help him. CSP 1, no. 435, p. 162.

6. 27 April 1550. Concerning 'the matter [dispute] between [Richard] Fulmerston and [William] Nawneton' [Naughton]. CSP 1, no. 438, p. 162.

7. 9 May 1550. Cautions against an 'arranged' marriage between her son and the Duke of Somerset's daughter. CSP 1, no. 439, pp. 162–3.

8. 18 May 1550. Seeks advice on how to approach the authorities with regard to her proposed purchase of Spilsby chantry. CSP 1, no. 441, p. 163.

9. 8 August 1550. Receives unspecified 'ill-favoured news'. CSP 1, no. 456, pp. 169–70.

10. 3 September 1550. Thanks Cecil for his help with William Naughton's 'matter' and proposes a further settlement. CSP 1, no. 459, p. 170.

11. 8 September 1550. Thanks Cecil for unspecified 'good news' received two days earlier. CSP 1, no. 460, pp. 170–1.

12. 18 September 1550. Again asks Cecil to use his influence to assist William Naughton. CSP 1, no. 467, p. 172.

13. 1 October 1550. Seeks arbitration in two local property disputes. CSP 1, no. 472, p. 172.

14. 2 October 1550. Seeks intervention on behalf of the brother of an unnamed person in a dispute with 'one of Jersey'. CSP 1, no. 473, p. 174.

15. 2 October 1550. Refers to commercial dealings with Cecil, and uses mercantile terminology to express relief that, after spending two months in the Tower after Somerset's fall, he has been restored to favour as a privy councillor and third Secretary of State. CSP 1, no. 474, p. 174.

16. 8 October 1550. Complains that Somerset has favoured Fulmerston against Naughton – hints at the malevolence of his duchess. CSP 1, no. 481, p. 175.

17. 15 November 1550. 'Help me to have the warrant for Spilsby Chantry we sued for.' Fears she will not be able to 'rule' her 'foolish choler' if Naughton does not receive justice. CSP 1, no. 488, pp. 177–8.

18. 19 November 1550. Naughton's case finally settled. Expresses her gratitude to Cecil and the Somersets and apologises for her 'coarseness in this matter'. CSP 1, no. 493, p. 179.

19. 17 February 1551. Asks Cecil to facilitate delivery of a letter written by Martin Bucer – 'why I require this you shall perceive from his letter, which he sends open'. CSP 1, no. 508, p. 193.

20. September 1551, Monday. 'I thank God for all His benefits, and take this last (at first sight most bitter) punishment not the least of them.' (Her two sons had died on 14 July.) CSP 1, no. 554, p. 206.

21. 13 May 1552. 'Weary with writing … Monson troubles me with complaints to the Lord Chancellor.' CSP 1, no. 618, p. 235. This was presumably Robert Monson, one of her Protestant

friends among the Lincolnshire gentry – it is unclear why they were at odds at this time.

22. June 1552, Wednesday 'in bed'. Sends Cecil a buck with an invitation to hunt. CSP 1, no. 669, pp. 243–4.

In Queen Elizabeth's reign:

23. 4 March 1559. From 'Crossen' (Crozen in Lithuania). Fears that the queen's commitment to Protestantism is only lukewarm and urges Cecil to promote the true faith. CSP 2, p. 123.

24. 30 October 1563. Thanks Cecil 'for his proffers of service; with a postscript from Richard Bertie refusing a public employment'. Lansdowne, Num. 6, 35, p. 16.

25. 9 August 1567. Complains that Lady Mary Grey has been sent to her without proper furniture, utensils, etc., and asks Cecil to persuade the queen to lend her some. CSP 2, p. 297.

26. 29 March 1569. Reminds Cecil of a suit made by a poor Dutchman who desires to bring his wife and goods to England, and reflects on the misery of those who suffer abroad for conscience sake. CSP 2, p. 332.

27. 8 October 1569. Thanks him for writing to inform her of the northern (Catholic) rebellion of the earls of Northumberland and Westmoreland; with a postscript from Richard Bertie. Lansdowne, Num. 11, 51, p. 27.

28. 29 July 1570. A long, indifferently spelt communication expressing her frustration that the queen has not advanced her husband to the barony of Willoughby or her son-in-law Reginald Grey to the earldom of Kent, and asking Cecil to deliver a letter to Her Majesty on her behalf. Salisbury, part 1, no. 1507, pp. 477–8.

29. 5 August 1570. Thanks Cecil for delivering her letter, and asks him 'to help to perfect what is well begun'. A postscript from

Richard Bertie emphasises that she fears her suits will fail unless her friends commend them to the queen. Salisbury, part 1, no. 1511, pp. 479–81.

30. 10 August 1570. Seeks Cecil's advice about when and where she should approach the queen in person. Salisbury, part 1, no. 1512, p. 481.

31. 1 September 1570. Richard Bertie thanks Cecil for his letters which have eased Katherine's 'extreme fits', and explains why he considers himself worthy to have the barony conferred on him. Salisbury, part 1, no. 1516, pp. 482–3.

32. 15 April 1571. Reports a discussion with the queen about Reginald Grey's claim to the earldom. CSP 2, p. 410.

33. April 1571. Thanks Cecil for his courteous enquiries after her health, and excuses herself for not having waited on the queen. CSP 2, p. 411

34. 2 May 1571. Reminds Cecil of their old friendship and asks him to do all he can to promote her son-in-law's claim to the earldom. CSP 2, p. 412.

35. 25 May 1571. Thanks Cecil for befriending Reginald Grey, but is perplexed by 'Her Majesty's strange countenance' towards her. CSP 2, p. 413.

36. 16 June 1571. Describes her most recent conversation with the queen and rejects what she calls 'common talk' that what she really wants is a 'high place' for Suzan. CSP 2, p. 415.

37. 30 June 1572. Asks Cecil to give Peregrine good counsel 'to bridle his youth', and to send him from court to his father. Lansdowne, Num. 28, 62, p. 64. (Misdated 1579 in the catalogue.)

38. 2 July 1577. Expresses reservations about her son Peregrine's wish to marry Mary de Vere with whom she has had a 'difficult' face-to-face conversation, and hopes Cecil (whose daughter was

unhappily married to Mary's brother, the Earl of Oxford) will use his influence to persuade the queen to forbid it. Salisbury, part 13, no. 202, pp. 146–7.

39. 14 July 1577. Encloses letter from Richard Bertie (who is away from home) expressing his opposition to the marriage, adding that she has not yet told her husband the full story of Peregrine's 'wilfulness and uncourteous dealings' with them. Salisbury, part 2, no. 464, p. 156.

40. 21 July 1577. Has heard that Cecil is on a journey, and is sorry she will not be able to thank him in person. Salisbury, part 2, no. 466, p. 156.

41. 15 December 1577. Proposes a plan to reconcile the Oxfords by encouraging the earl to become fond of their child. Lansdowne, Num. 25, 27, p. 57.

42. 12 March 1578. Asks Cecil to do her several favours, including granting her son and daughter-in-law a bill 'of impost' for two tuns of wine to be taken at Hull or Boston. Salisbury, part 2, no. 505, p. 173.

43. 23 September 1579. Assures Cecil that although ill she is not 'altogether senseless' as a foolish servant of hers had led him to think. Lansdowne, Num. 28, no. 65, p. 64.

44. 4 April 1580 (Easter Monday). Asks Cecil to obtain the queen's permission for Peregrine to travel abroad. Lansdowne, Num. 30, 39, p. 68.

Appendix 2

PORTRAITS OF KATHERINE WILLOUGHBY

The best known image of Katherine is the miniature after Hans Holbein the Younger, painted in her early womanhood. In a second portrait at Grimsthorpe dated 1548, three years after she was widowed, she is soberly dressed and her demeanour is altogether more serious. The bust on her monument at Spilsby (which is more finely carved than the rest of the edifice and may have been intended for another location) shows her in her old age.

Another three-quarter-length portrait at Grimsthorpe (not illustrated) depicts a lady who has been variously identified as Mary, Queen of Scots and Lady Jane Dudley (Jane Grey). It is clearly not of Mary, and Jane's name has been attached to a number of paintings, none of which can be authenticated. A detailed scientific analysis of the work could help to identify the sitter, but there is no likelihood of this being undertaken in the near future. All we can say is that this lady's features very closely resemble those of Katherine in her other portraits.

There is also a drawing of 'The Dutchess of Suffolk' by Holbein now in the Royal Collection. Holbein returned to England in

1531, so the person depicted could be the then duchess, Mary, Henry VIII's sister, who died in 1533, or Frances, Katherine's stepdaughter, if the suggestion that the captions were not added until between 1555 and 1557 is accurate. No conclusions can be drawn from the sitter's apparent age because Katherine was actually two years younger than Frances. All we can say is that Katherine, who was Duchess of Suffolk from 1533 to 1545 (before becoming dowager duchess), is perhaps a more likely candidate than the other two.

NOTES AND REFERENCES

Prologue: A Most Remarkable Letter

1. Transcribed from a letter in the possession of Mr Charles Cottrell Dormer of Rousham, Oxfordshire, and previously printed by Lady Cecilie Goff in *A Woman of the Tudor Age* (1930), pp. 315–6. I have modernised the spelling.

1 Childhood, 1519–1533

1. The descent of the baronies of Willoughby and Wells is fully described in G. E. Cokayne *et al.*, *The Complete Peerage*, xii, part 2 (1959).
2. Luis Caroz de Villaragut, Spanish Ambassador in England to Friar Juan de Eztuniga, Provincial of Aragon, 6 December 1514. *Calendar of Letters, Despatches and State Papers relating to the Negotiations between England and Spain, Preserved in the archives at Simancas and elsewhere*, vol. ii, Henry VIII 1509–1525, ed. G. A. Bergenroth (1866), no. 201, p. 248.
3. These figures are taken from J. Guy, *Tudor England* (Oxford, 1988), pp. 32 & 38. Similarly, agricultural prices as represented by 100 in the period 1450–1499 had reached 115 by 1519 and 154 a decade later, p. 35.
4. Historical Manuscripts Commission, *Report on the Manuscripts of the Earl of Ancaster preserved at Grimsthorpe* (1907), p. 468.

5. The Willoughby inheritance dispute was extremely complicated, and I have here reduced it to its bare essentials. For a fuller discussion see M. F. Harkrider, 'Women, Reform and Community in Early Modern England: Katherine Willoughby, Duchess of Suffolk, and Lincolnshire's Godly Aristocracy, 1519–1580'. *Studies in Modern British Religious History* (2008), pp. 33–5.

6. S. J. Gunn, *Charles Brandon, Duke of Suffolk, c. 1484–1545* (1988), p. 1.

7. His objections were mere technicalities – that his grandmother had been related to Dame Margaret's first husband, for example – but they were sufficient to annul a marriage at that time.

8. British Library Cotton MS Caligula D. vi, fol. 186r, quoted by S. J. Gunn in his article on Brandon in the *Oxford Dictionary of National Biography*, ed. H. C. G. Matthew & B. Harrison, 60 vols (Oxford, 2004), vol. 7, p. 355.

9. The relevant passages are Leviticus, chapter 18, verse 16, and chapter 20, verse 21, and Deuteronomy, chapter 25, verse 5. The quotation is from Luke, chapter 20, verse 28.

10. *Letters and Papers, Foreign and Domestic, of the Reign of Henry VIII*, vol. vi, ed. J. Gairdner (1882), no. 1558, p. 628.

11. Frances and Henry Grey were married between 28 July 1533 and 4 February 1534, so the ceremony would have taken place after Mary's death but could have been before or after Brandon's marriage to Katherine.

12. These paragraphs are based on the description of the funeral in M. A. E Green, *Lives of the Princesses of England from the Norman Conquest*, 6 vols (1849–1855), v, pp. 138–141.

13. According to Anthony Martienssen, Katherine was educated at court by the Valencian humanist scholar Juan Luis Vives, who had been employed to tutor the seven-year-old Princess Mary and the nine-year-old Catherine Parr in 1523. He maintains that other girls, including Frances and Eleanor Brandon, Joan Guildford (the daughter of another lady-in-waiting), and Katherine herself were added to the class as they reached a similar age, but unfortunately does not give the source of his information (*Queen Katherine*

Parr (1975), p. 31). Linda Porter, whose authoritative study of the queen was published in 2010, states plainly that 'we do not know who Katherine Parr's tutors were or precisely what she studied' (*Katherine the Queen: The Remarkable Life of Katherine Parr*, p. 34).

2 The Brandon Marriage, 1533–1545

1. *Spanish Calendar*, vol. iv, part 2, Henry VIII, 1531–1533, ed. P de Gayangos (1882), no. 1123, pp. 788–9.
2. S. J. Gunn, *Charles Brandon*, p. 176.
3. *Ibid*. Chapuys was writing to the Emperor on Wednesday 3 September. 'Next Sunday' was the 7th.
4. Alison Sim, *The Tudor Housewife* (Stroud, 1996), chapter 4.
5. Brandon worked hard at this, but was never able to recover some 22 per cent of the former de la Pole estate. See Gunn, *Charles Brandon*, p. 42.
6. *Letters and Papers Henry VIII*, vol. x, ed. J. Gairdner (1887), no. 284, p. 106. There was a story that Lady Maria was subsequently buried with Queen Catherine, but no second body was discovered when the grave was opened in 1884.
7. Charles Wriothesley, *A Chronicle of England During the Reigns of the Tudors, from A.D. 1485 to 1559*, ed. W. D. Hamilton, 2 vols (Camden Society, 1875 & 1877), i, pp. 50–1.
8. Local rivalries also played a part in the troubles. It can hardly be coincidence that many of Christopher Willoughby's supporters joined the rebellion – his heir, William, even served as 'Grand Captain' of the Horncastle contingent – but Lady Maria Willoughby's servants and clients did not.
9. *Letters and Papers Henry VIII*, vol. xi, ed. J. Gairdner (1888), no. 650, p. 255 & no. 1267, p. 517.
10. Melissa F. Harkrider has calculated that Katherine's network encompassed kinship relationships with twenty gentry families in Lincolnshire and East Anglia, patronage ties with seventy-three

families in Lincolnshire and at court, and fifty-five ecclesiastical contacts in this region. *Women, Reform and Community*, p. 19.

11. Quoted by Linda Porter in *Katherine the Queen*, p. 50.

12. Honor, Lady Lisle to her husband, 15 November 1538. *The Lisle Letters*, ed. M. St C. Byrne, 6 vols (Chicago, 1981), v, no. 1270, p. 283. Robert Warner informed Lord Fitzwater that 'on the Wednesday before he [the king] made a banquet, at which were the Duke of Suffolk and his wife, my lord my master, and my lady [the Earl and Countess of Sussex], the Earl of Hertford and his wife, and my Lady Lisle, with other maids that were the queen's women. They lay all night in court and had banquets in their chambers, and the king's servants to wait upon them, and did not take their leave till four o'clock after dinner next day.' *Letters and Papers Henry VIII*, vol. xiii, part 2, ed. J Gairdner (1893), no. 884, p. 369. Prince Edward's christening is described in H. W. Chapman, *The Last Tudor King* (1958), pp. 28–9.

13. Leanda de Lisle explains that 'The term Protestant only began to be used in England in the mid–1550s. The more usual term for those we would now think of as Protestant was 'evangelical'. They were so named because they wishes to return to the 'evangelium' or 'good news' of the gospel, stripping away church traditions they believed had no biblical basis in favour of a more fundamental reading of scripture'. *The Sisters Who Would Be Queen. The Tragedy of Mary, Katherine and Lady Jane Grey* (2010), p. 17.

14. These particulars are taken from C. D. C. Armstrong's article on Gardiner in the *Oxford Dictionary of National Biography*, vol. 21, pp. 433–445.

15. The Protestant divine Hugh Latimer argued that no one could earn salvation, rather, 'our saviour teacheth us that we can do nothing of ourselves ... [he] merited the kingdom of heaven for us through his most painful death and passion'. Quoted by Melissa Harkrider, *Women, Reform and Community*, p. 54.

16. Gunn, *Charles Brandon*, pp. 229 & 164.

17. Quoted by Melissa Harkrider in *Women, Reform and Community*, p. 43.

18. Quoted by Evelyn Read in *Catherine, Duchess of Suffolk: A Portrait* (1962), pp. 54–5.

19. One of his favourite targets was purgatory which is never mentioned by name in the Bible – but Henry told him bluntly that his arguments were based on 'carnal wit' and that 'purgatory may yet stand'.

20. This paragraph is based on Susan Wabuda's article on Latimer in the *Oxford Dictionary of National Biography*, vol. xxxii, pp. 632–9. Henry's 'toleration of doctrinal innovation waned with shocking suddenness' she writes, and the Six Articles 'represented an almost complete return to a traditional understanding of the nature of the Eucharist [the 'real presence'], and a tacit recognition that masses benefited the departed'.

21. Martienssen, *Queen Katherine Parr*, p. 143.

22. This is an estimate. Catherine Parr was born in 1512, Catherine Howard at some time between 1518 and 1524, probably nearer the latter date.

23. See Harkrider, *Women, Reform and Community*, p. 49, on which this paragraph is based.

24. *Wills From Doctors' Commons*, ed. J. G. Nichols & J. Bruce (Camden Society, 1863), pp. 33–4, 37. Gunn, *Charles Brandon*, p. 208. I am grateful to Nicola Tallis for checking the original of this for me.

25. Quoted in *Ibid.*, p. 221, and in Gunn's article on Brandon in *The Oxford Dictionary of National Biography*, vol. vii, p. 357.

26. Quoted in *Ibid.*, p. 70.

27. Edward Halle, *The Union of the Two Noble and Illustrious Families of Lancaster and York* (1550, reprinted Menston, 1970), The xxxvii year of King Henry the Eighth, folio cclx.

3 King Henry's Last Love, 1545–1547

1. Quoted by Melissa Harkrider in *Women, Reform and Community*, p. 50.

2. John Strype, *Annals,* ii, part 2, p. 347, quoted by Evelyn Read in

Catherine, Duchess of Suffolk: A Portrait, p. 52. The translation is by Professor Kenneth Setton of the University of Pennsylvania.

3. *The Lisle Letters*, iv, no. 871, p. 128. National Archives Lisle Papers (S.P.3, xi, no. 103). *Letters and Papers Henry VIII*, vol. xii, 1, ed. J. Gairdner (1890), no. 680, pp. 298–9.

4. *The Lisle Letters*, iv, no. 854a, p. 70.

5. *Ibid.*, iv, no. 901, p. 178. Katherine Bassett was by this time in Lady Rutland's service.

6. *Ibid.*, v, no. 1409, p. 474.

7. *Ibid.*, v, no. 1423, p. 485; no. 1436, p. 512. See also nos. 1420, 1425, 1427 & 1453.

8. Katherine asked that the wine be sent to her husband, but he then sent two-thirds of it to her – a nice touch.

9. *Ibid.*, v, no. 1457a, p. 543.

10. *Ibid.*, v, no. 1525, p. 634.

11. *The Lisle Letters*, v, no. 1526, pp. 634–5. *British Library Cotton MS. Vespasian* F. xiii, f.154. *Letters and Papers Henry VIII*, vol. vii, ed. J. Gairdner (1883), no. 1080, p. 419.

12. Quoted by Melissa Harkrider in *Women, Reform and Community*, pp. 54 & 79.

13. *The Acts and Monuments of John Foxe* (4th edn, 1877), ed. J. Pratt, viii, p. 570.

14. *Spanish Calendar*, vol. viii., Henry VIII, 1546–1547, ed. M. A. S. Hume (1904), no. 386, p. 555.

15. *Ibid.*, no. 204, p. 318.

16. Quoted by Anthony Martienssen, *Queen Katherine Parr*, p. 210.

17. *Letters and Papers Henry VIII*, vol. xiii, part 1, ed. J. Gairdner (1892), no. 583, p. 215. *Spanish Calendar*, vol. v, part 2, Henry VIII, 1536–1538, ed. P. de Gayangos (1888), no. 220, p. 520.

18. Although Brandon's biographer, S. J. Gunn, attributes this reward to his recent good service in France. *The Oxford Dictionary of National Biography*, www.oxforddnb.com/view/printable/3260.

19. Chapuys to the Queen of Hungary, 8 January 1541. *Spanish Calendar*, vol. vi, part 1, Henry VIII 1538–1542, ed. P. de Gayangos (1890), pp. 305–6.

20. Foxe, *Acts and Monuments*, v, p. 547.

21. *Ibid.*, pp. 555–560.

22. Goff, *A Woman of the Tudor Age*, p. 167. *Spanish Calendar*, vol. ix, Edward VI, 1547–1549, ed. M. A. S. Hume & R. Turner (1912), p. 88–9.

23. *Calendar of State Papers Domestic Series, Edward VI 1547–1553*, ed. C. S. Knighton (revised edn, 1992), no. 41.

4 Tragedy, 1547–1553

1. The question of how far Henry was aware of this 'unfulfilled gifts' clause is discussed in Chris Skidmore's *Edward VI: The Lost King of England* (2008), pp. 45–48.

2. The letter is transcribed in Goff, *A Woman of the Tudor Age*, pp. 172–3. The full title of the queen's book was *The lamentatio[n] of a sinner, made by the most vertuous Lady Queen Katherin, bewailing the ignorance of her blinde life, set foorth and put in print at the instaunt desire of the right gratious Lady Katherin Duches of Suffolke, and the ernest request of the right honorable Lord William Parr, Marquesse of Northampton.*

3. Grimsthorpe, 24 July 1549. National Archives State Papers Domestic 10/8/35. Read, *Catherine, Duchess of Suffolk*, p. 72.

4. 27 August 1549. British Library Lansdowne MSS No. 2, part 17. Goff, *A Woman of the Tudor Age*, p. 175–6. Linda Porter adds that 'Even allowing for the duchess's pecuniary embarrassment (which may have been exaggerated, as was common at the time), it is a thoroughly unpleasant epistle. The picture it paints of an unwanted child, her anxious servants unpaid, and her guardian describing her as a sickness, does the Duchess of Suffolk little credit.' *Katherine the Queen*, p. 342.

5. *Ibid.*, Goff, pp. 176–7.

6. HMC, *Ancaster*, p. 453.

7. *Ibid.*, p. 457.

8. Goff, *A Woman of the Tudor Age*, p. 186 & p. 175. *CSP Edward VI*, nos 205, 429, 430, 474, 512.

9. John Strype, *Ecclesiastical Memorials* (1721), ii, part 1, p. 83, quoted by Evelyn Read in *Catherine, Duchess of Suffolk*, pp. 66–7.

10. Harkrider, *Women, Reform and Community*, pp. 53–4.

11. Foxe, *Acts and Monuments*, v, p. 570. Goff, *A Woman of the Tudor Age*, p. 179.

12. These particulars are taken from Harkrider, *Women, Reform and Community*, p. 125.

13. *CSP Edward VI*, no. 435.

14. *Ibid.*, no. 439

15. *Ibid.*, no. 481.

16. (Thomas) Wilson, *Arte of Rhetorique*, ed. G. H. Mair (Oxford, 1909), p. 15.

17. *Ibid.*, quoting Wordsworth's *Ecclesiastical Biography*.

18. Quoted by Lady Goff in *A Woman of the Tudor Age*, p. 187

19. B. Hall, 'Martin Bucer in England', *Martin Bucer: Reforming Church and Community*, ed. D. F. Wright (Cambridge, 1994), p. 146. Katherine's close personal attachment to Bucer is evident in a letter she wrote to William Cecil on 17 February 1551 – 'At Bucer's request and partly for my own commodity I ask you to see this his letter enclosed speedily delivered. If you cannot help, advise the bearer how it may be done. Why I require this you shall perceive from his letter, which he sends open. Considering his sickness, give it more than I am worth.' *CSP, Edward VI*, no. 508.

20. The disease vanished as abruptly as it had appeared. The last reported outbreak was in 1578.

21. Wilson, *Arte of Rhetorique*, p. 68.

22. *Ibid.*, pp. 14–16.

23. *Ibid.*, p. 66.

24. *Ibid.*, pp. 75–6, & p. 84.

25. We may wonder how far Katherine was consoled by arguments such as 'If your children were alive, and by the advice of some wicked person, were brought to a brothel house, where enticing harlots lived, and so were in danger to commit that foul sin of whoredom, and so led from one wickedness to another'. But they have been delivered 'from this present evil world, which I count

none other than a brothel house, and a life of all naughtiness'. *Ibid.*, pp. 72–3.

26. H. Robinson (trans & ed.), *Original Letters Relative to the English Reformation written during the reigns of King Henry VIII, King Edward VI, and Queen Mary, chiefly from the archives of Zurich*, 2 vols (Cambridge,1846–7), ii, p. 496.

27. *Ibid.*, pp. 84–5.

28. Goff, *A Woman of the Tudor Age*, p. 184. *CSP Edward VI*, nos. 438, 441, 472, 473, 459, 467, 481, 488, 493.

29. *CSP Edward VI*, no. 554. Read, *Catherine, Duchess of Suffolk*, pp. 85–6.

30. *CSP Edward VI*, no. 669. Read, *Catherine, Duchess of Suffolk*, p.88.

31. *Ibid.*

32. Katherine's stepdaughter Frances (Brandon) followed her example when she wed her groom, Adrian Stokes, in March 1555, just over a year after her first husband's execution.

33. Wilson, *Arte of Rhetorique*, p. 15.

34. David Cressy has estimated that 90 per cent of London women and perhaps 95 per cent of those who resided outside the capital could not write at this period. See S. W. Hull, *Chaste, Silent and Obedient: English Books for Women 1475–1640* (1988), p. 4.

35. Sim, *The Tudor Housewife*, p. 39.

36. This paragraph is based on Skidmore, *Edward VI*, especially pp. 197–8 & 231–2.

5 The Bid for the Throne, 1553–1554

* My summary of the Lady Jane Grey conspiracy is drawn from several contemporary and modern sources, all of which differ in matters of detail. In all cases of doubt I have used the version which, on balance, seemed most likely to be true.

1. Although Nicola Tallis argues for an earlier date, perhaps June 1536 (personal communication).

2. Northumberland's elder sons were married already. One of them was Robert Dudley, who was later to become Queen Elizabeth's great favourite but whose life could have ended on the block had he been single in 1553.

3. One source says that Katherine was sent to reside with her in-laws at Baynard's Castle – but she and her husband did not live together as man and wife.

4. H. W. Chapman, *Lady Jane Grey* (1962), p. 70.

5. Alison Plowden, *Lady Jane Grey and the House of Suffolk* (1985), p. 87, quoting the Venetian envoy Giulio Raviglio Rosso.

6. It is worth pointing out that if Mary and Elizabeth *were* illegitimate, then whom they married no longer mattered. But it is possible that Edward been planning to deny the crown to Mary (who he feared would undo his religious settlement) for some time.

7. The phrase is Hester Chapman's, *Lady Jane Grey* (1962), p. 109. According to the *Chronicle of the Grey Friars of London*, ed. J. G. Nichols (Camden Society, 1852), p. 78, Ridley called both Mary and Elizabeth bastards whereupon 'alle the pepull was sore anoyd with hys worddes, so uncherytabulle spokyne by hym in soo opyne ane awdiens'.

8. Noted by Eric Ives, *Lady Jane Grey: A Tudor Mystery* (Wiley-Blackwell, 2011), p. 189.

9. A potentially decisive factor was that Northumberland assumed that Mary's men would be no match for his artillery, and it was only when he reached Bury that he learned that she had acquired cannon too.

10. Foxe, *Acts and Monuments*, vi, pp. 390 & 419.

11. *The Chronicle of Queen Jane and of two years of Queen Mary*, ed. J. G. Nichols (Camden Society, 1850), pp. 19 & 25.

12. Quoted by Hester Chapman, *Lady Jane Grey*, p. 169.

13. *Spanish Calendar*, vol. 12, Mary, January–July 1554, ed. Royall Tyler (1949), p. 87.

14. Foxe, *Acts and Monuments*, vi, p. 416. There can be little doubt that a conversation like the one recorded by Foxe took place, but, as on other occasions, he must be viewed with caution.

15. Quoted by Leanda de Lisle in *The Sisters Who Would Be Queen*, p. 147.
16. *Chronicle of Queen Jane*, p. 54.

6 Escape, 1554–1555

1. A later version was that Cecil had signed only as a witness, but Eric Ives describes him as 'Northumberland's right-hand man'. In Ives's opinion, 'the most charitable view of his excuses is that, to save his skin, he was decidedly "economical with the truth"'. *Lady Jane Grey*, pp. 164–5.
2. This paragraph is based on Susan Wabuda's article in the *Oxford DNB*.
3. All these quotations are taken from Foxe, *Acts and Monuments*, viii, pp. 569–71.
4. This paragraph is based on Thomas S. Freeman's article in the *Oxford DNB*.
5. Project Canterbury. http://anglicanhistory.org/reformation/ps/ridley/letters22-34.pdf. This letter is no. 25. The value of the royal, or ryall, varied. It is said to have been worth 11s 3d in 1 Henry VIII, 13s 6d in 2 Edward VI, and 15s in 2 Elizabeth I.
6. Foxe, *Acts and Monuments*, viii, p. 571.
7. The Barbican, later called Willoughby House (probably to distinguish it from the street called Barbican), had belonged to Katherine's parents. Lady Goff refers to an 'old print' of Katherine setting out on her journey preserved in the Ashmolean Museum which depicts the Barbican as 'a large, square, embattled building, with a cupola surmounted by a cross at each corner and a large flag, bearing the Ufford cross, in the centre of the building'. But there is no date or indication of how 'imaginative' the reconstruction might be.
8. Foxe, *Acts and Monuments*, viii, pp. 571–2.
9. *Ibid.*, p. 572.
10. *Ibid.*
11. Goff, *A Woman of the Tudor Age*, p. 226. No reference is given for this statement, and I have been unable to trace the source.

12. Foxe, *Acts and Monuments*, viii, p. 572.
13. *Ibid.* British Library Additional MSS 33271, ff. 9v–10, quoted by Melissa Harkrider in *Women, Reform and Community*, p. 104.

7 Exile, 1555–1559

1. Foxe, *Acts and Monuments*, viii, p. 572.
2. The Protestant inhabitants of French Flanders.
3. Foxe, *Acts and Monuments*, viii, p. 573. Katherine had supported Perusell financially and politically when he had been minister of the French Strangers' Church in London.
4. *Ibid.*
5. Landsknechts were European mercenary soldiers, feared for their rapacity and brutality.
6. Foxe, *Acts and Monuments*, viii, p. 573.
7. *Ibid.*, pp. 574.
8. *Ibid.* Read, *Catherine, Duchess of Suffolk*, p. 113.
9. See Alison Weir, *Elizabeth of York. The First Tudor Queen* (2013), p. 228. We have to assume that Peregrine was a full-term baby. Recent studies have suggested that gestation can vary by up to five weeks.
10. Foxe, *Acts and Monuments*, viii, p. 574.
11. Goff, *A Woman of the Tudor Age*, p. 229. The ambassador was Charles Bertie and the year was 1681.
12. The term 'ensign' usually refers to an individual junior officer, but Lady Bertie suggests that in this instance it should be read as 'enseignes', meaning battalions or companies. Lady Georgina Bertie, *Five Generations of a Loyal House Pt. 1, Containing the Lives of R. Bertie and His Son Peregrine, Lord Willoughby* (Rivingtons, 1845; reprinted ULAN, 2012), p. 29.
13. Harkrider, *Women, Reform and Community*, p. 103. For the exile community's forms of government and worship see pp. 102–3.
14. Read, *Catherine, Duchess of Suffolk*, p. 121. Harkrider, *Women, Reform and Community*, pp. 110–11.
15. A palsgrave is defined as 'a count or earl who has the overseeing

of a prince's palace'. Samuel Johnson, *A Dictionary of the English Language*, 2 vols (1824), ii, p. 272.

16. John Brett, 'A Narrative of the Pursuit of English Refugees in Germany under Queen Mary', ed. I. S. Leadham, *Transactions of the Royal Historical Society*, New Series, xi (1897), pp. 122–9.

17. *Women, Reform and Community*, p. 107.

18. *Remains of Myles Coverdale, Bishop of Exeter*, ed. G. Pearson, Parker Society (Cambridge, 1846), letter xxxv, pp. 527–8. The letter has been assigned to 20 September 1543 (probably because Coverdale had previously worked at Bad Bergzabern as a schoolmaster between 1543 and 1547), but this is unlikely on several counts: Coverdale did not live in Wesel at this period, and Charles Brandon, Katherine's then husband, was serving as king's lieutenant in the north of England between January 1543 and March 1544. He also writes that she 'owed' nothing to Bucer rather than 'owes'. There is therefore no reason to doubt the accuracy of Pearson's revised date.

19. Francis Guevara was the son of Katherine's mother's sister Inez de Salinas. He was subsequently rewarded with an annuity of £30 charged on their estates.

20. Katherine and Bertie controlled their income to the extent that they were able to instruct Herenden and Alice Bertie to repay creditors, but government attempts to prevent monies reaching them inevitably reduced their resources. Bertie and Herenden discussed the best means of sending funds to them without provoking the Crown's anger. Harkrider, *Women, Reform and Community*, p. 109.

21. Although Melissa Harkrider says that Lord William 'nearly succeeded in winning them'. *Women, Reform and Community*, p. 107.

22. Strictly speaking, Sigismund II Augustus only became King of Poland on his father's death in 1548, but had been his co-regent since 1529.

23. Foxe, *Acts and Monuments*, viii, p. 574.

24. This is a mistake. Barlow was Bishop of Bath and Wells from 1548 to 1553 – he did not become Bishop of Chichester until 1559.

25. Foxe, *Acts and Monuments*, viii, p. 574–5.

26. *Ibid.*, p. 576.

27. Both Lady Goff and Mrs Read refer obliquely to these presents, but neither gives a reference.
28. National Archives, State Papers Domestic, 12/2/10. Transcribed by Lady Georgina Bertie in *Five Generations of a Loyal House*, pp. 34–5.
29. National Archives. State Papers Domestic. 12/3/9. Letter dated 4 March 1559.
30. *Certain Godly Sermons, made upon the Lord's Prayer, preached by the right reverend father and constant martyr of Christ, Master Hugh Latimer, before the right honourable and virtuous Lady Katherine, Duchess of Suffolk, in the year of Our Lord 1553*, gathered and collected by Augustine Bernher (1562). From Bernher's introduction (no pagination).
31. Quoted by Mrs Read in *Catherine, Duchess of Suffolk*, p. 129.

8 Lady of the Manor, 1559–1565

1. *Calendar of the Patent Rolls, Elizabeth I 1558–1560* (1939), p. 25. National Archives, State Papers Domestic, 12/6/2.
2. College of Arms, Arundel, no. 35, ff. 5–9, quoted by Leanda de Lisle in *The Sisters Who Would be Queen*, p. 196 & note 10.
3. British Library Lansdowne MSS 35, no. 90. Read, *Catherine, Duchess of Suffolk*, p. 167.
4. Lincolnshire Archives, Ancaster MSS, v/B/4. See also Historical Manuscripts Commission, *Report on the Manuscripts of the Earl of Ancaster preserved at Grimsthorpe* (1907), pp. 459–473.
5. Mentioned in Henry Machyn's diary, *The Diary of Henry Machyn A.D. 1550–1563*, ed. J. G. Nichols (Camden Society, 1848), p. 308. Machyn blames 'a French man that kept the place' and notes that 'a part burned'.
6. The accounts are Lincolnshire Archives, Ancaster MSS, vii/A/2. See also Historical Manuscripts Commission, *Report on the Manuscripts of the Earl of Ancaster preserved at Grimsthorpe* (1907), pp. 459–473.

7. David Daniell, 'Miles Coverdale 1488–1569', www.oxforddnb.com/view/article/6486.

8. A simple purchasing power calculator would say that the relative value is £6,303, the percentage increase in the RPI between 1560 and 2013, but a calculation based on economic power considerations gives a figure of £1,883,000. www.measuringworth.com/ukcompare/relativevalue.php.

9. Edmund Hall, described as 'earnest in religion' entered Katherine's service in the 1540s and subsequently sat in Parliament. During Elizabeth I's reign, he handled her property disputes, and sent her gifts in recognition of her patronage. See Harkrider, *Women, Reform and Community*, p. 122.

10. Grogram was a coarse, often stiffened fabric made from silk, mohair or wool or a combination of them.

11. In *The Alchemist*, Ben Jonson alleges masters regularly sought to rid themselves of devalued currency by paying their servants with it.

12. Lincolnshire Archives, Ancaster MSS, vii/A/5.

13. 'The 'Abbot of Unreason' (suppressed in 1555) had a similar role in Scotland, while a 'Boy Bishop' led the children's Christmas festivities in the choir schools. The court ceased to appoint a Lord of Misrule after Edward VI's death, and the practice was abolished in the reign of James I.

14. The shorter distances covered on the first two days leave the question of precisely what form of transportation was used open, but Katherine would almost certainly have been mounted in order to cover approximately fifty miles on the third.

15. Goff, *A Woman of the Tudor Age*, p. 272.

9 A Bed of Nails, 1565–1580

1. *Calendar of Letters and State Papers relating to English Affairs preserved in the archives at Simancas and elsewhere*, vol. 1 Elizabeth, 1558–1567, ed. M. A. S. Hume (1892), p. 468.

2. Strictly speaking, they were first cousins once removed.

3. Whatever Mary's misdeeds, she was still a relative of the queen, and had been allowed to retain the services of a waiting woman and a groom.

4. National Archives, 12/43/40. Read, *Catherine, Duchess of Suffolk*, pp. 143–5.

5. Mary's appointment as a 'Maid' surely reflects Elizabeth's reluctance to accept that she had been a married woman.

6. Historical Manuscripts Commission, *Calendar of the Manuscripts of the Marquis of Salisbury preserved at Hatfield House, Hertfordshire*, part 1 (1883), no. 1507, pp. 477–8.

7. *Ibid.*, pp. 479–80.

8. *Ibid.*, pp. 482–3.

9. *Ibid.*, p. 481.

10. National Archives, 12/78/18. *CSP Domestic 1547–1580*, p. 413.

11. National Archives, 12/78/42. *CSP Domestic 1547–1580*, p. 415.

12. Quoted by Leanda de Lisle in *The Sisters Who Would Be Queen*, p. 277.

13. M. A. R. Groves, *Burghley: William Cecil, Lord Burghley* (1998), p. 4. Groves points to an anonymous biographer who records that Cecil's work as a judge 'drew upon him such multitudes of suits as was incredible ... there was not a day in a term wherein he received not threescore, fourscore, and an hundred petitions, which he commonly read that night, and gave every man answer himself the next morning ... [and that] besides foreign letters, he received not so few as 20 or 30 other letters in a day', p. 5.

14. All these examples are taken from *A Catalogue of the Lansdowne Manuscripts in the British Museum* (British Museum Department of Manuscripts, 1819, reprinted 2012), pp. 24–29.

15. *CSP Domestic 1547–1580*, pp. 316 & 406.

16. British Library Additional MSS 48043, fol. 1–9. Bertie refuted Knox's arguments one by one, arguing that he was inconsistent and sometimes contradicted himself. It was never published, nor is there any indication that it was seen by the queen.

17. The letter is dated 1579 in the Lansdowne MSS catalogue, but the last digit is obscure and could be read as a 2. Peregrine would have

been twenty-three in June 1579, an age at which the stricture would have made little sense.

18. Salisbury MSS, part xiii [addenda] (1915), pp. 146–7. Mrs Read assumes that Katherine was worried that the young couple would marry without obtaining the queen's permission and wanted Cecil to do his utmost to ensure that consent was forthcoming; but the implication is surely that she saw Elizabeth's refusal as her last line of defence.
19. *Ibid.*, part ii (1888), p. 156.
20. *HMC Ancaster*, p. 4.
21. Salisbury MSS, part ii (1888), p. 156.
22. Lansdowne MSS 25, no. 27. Read, *Catherine, Duchess of Suffolk*, pp. 184–5.
23. Salisbury MSS, part ii (1888), p. 173.
24. *Ibid.*, p. 205.
25. Lansdowne MSS 25, no. 39. Read, *Catherine, Duchess of Suffolk*, pp. 189–190.
26. For a more detailed discussion of this see Melissa Harkrider, *Women, Reform and Community*, chapter 6. As early as 1547 the reformer John Olde had attributed the advancement of Protestantism in Lincolnshire to the 'helping forwardness of that devout woman of God, the Duchess of Suffolk'. *Ibid.*, p. 75, quoting Strype, *Ecclesiastical Memorials*, vol. 2, pt. 1, p. 83.
27. *CSP Domestic 1547–1580*, p. 316. Goff, *A Woman of the Tudor Age*, p. 285.
28. Salisbury MSS, part i (1883), p. 482.
29. *CSP Domestic 1547–1580*, p. 411. Read, *Catherine, Duchess of Suffolk*, p. 174.
30. Lansdowne MSS 28, no. 65. Read, *Ibid.*, p. 188.

Postscript: The Ravages of Time

1. *HMC Ancaster*, p. 5.
2. It would be reasonable to suppose that Katherine had known Lady

Zouche and Lady Wray as well as she knew Mildred Cecil, but no correspondence or record of her dealings with them survives.

3. Lincolnshire Archives, Mon/27/3/1, pp. 312–5. (Copied from Ashmolean MSS 836, fol. 256.)

4. I am grateful to Nicola Tallis for discussing the etiquette of these occasions with me. It may be noted that Lady Jane Grey acted as chief mourner at Queen Catherine Parr's funeral, and that Catherine Grey did likewise when her mother Frances was buried. The widowers, Thomas Seymour and Adrian Stokes, played no part.

5. Quoted by Maurice Howard in *The Early Tudor Country House: Architecture and Politics 1490–1550* (1987), p. 132.

6. N. Pevsner, *The Buildings of England: Suffolk* (Harmondsworth, 1961), p. 361.

7. Maurice Howard suggests that Brandon was seeking to equal or surpass the house which the Thimelby family had recently built at Irnham, a few miles away. *The Early Tudor Country House*, p. 32.

SELECT BIBLIOGRAPHY

The place of publication is London unless otherwise stated.

Bertie, Lady Georgina, *Five Generations of a Loyal House Pt. 1, Containing the Lives of R. Bertie and His Son Peregrine, Lord Willoughby* (Rivingtons, 1845; reprinted ULAN, 2012).

Brett, John, 'A Narrative of the Pursuit of English Refugees in Germany under Queen Mary', ed. I. S. Leadham, *Transactions of the Royal Historical Society*, New Series, xi (1897).

British Library, Lansdowne Manuscripts, Additional Manuscripts.

Byrne, Muriel St Clare (ed.), *The Lisle Letters*, 6 vols (Chicago, 1981).

Calendar of Letters, Despatches and State Papers relating to the Negotiations between England and Spain, Preserved in the archives at Simancas and elsewhere, vol. ii, Henry VIII 1509–1525, ed. G. A. Bergenroth (1866); vol. iv, part 2, Henry VIII, 1531–1533, ed. P. de Gayangos (1882); vol. v, part 2, Henry VIII 1536–1538, ed. P. de Gayangos (1888); vol. vi, part 1, Henry VIII 1538–1542, ed. P. de Gayangos (1890); vol. viii, Henry VIII, 1545–1546, ed. M. A. S Hume (1904); vol. ix, Edward VI, 1547–1549, ed. M. A. S. Hume & R Tyler (1912); vol. xii, Mary, January–July 1554, ed. Royall Tyler (1949).

Calendar of Letters and State Papers relating to English Affairs preserved principally in the Archives of Simancas, vol. 1 Elizabeth 1558–1567, ed. M. A. S. Hume (1892).

Calendar of State Papers Domestic Series, Edward VI, Mary, Elizabeth, 1547–1580, ed. R. Lemon (1856).

Calendar of State Papers Domestic Series, Edward VI 1547–1553, ed. C. S. Knighton (revised edn, 1992).

Catalogue of the Lansdowne Manuscripts in the British Museum (British Museum Department of Manuscripts, 1819; reprinted 2012).

Certain Godly Sermons, made upon the Lord's Prayer, preached by the right reverend father and constant martyr of Christ, Master Hugh Latimer, before the right honourable and virtuous Lady Katherine, Duchess of Suffolk, in the year of Our Lord 1553, gathered and collected by Augustine Bernher (1562).

Chapman, Hester W., *Lady Jane Grey* (1962).

Chapman, Hester W., *The Last Tudor King: A Study of Edward VI* (1958).

The Chronicle of the Grey Friars of London, ed. J. G. Nichols (Camden Society, 1852).

The Chronicle of Queen Jane and of Two Years of Queen Mary, ed. J. G. Nichols (Camden Society, 1850).

Collinson, Patrick, *The Elizabethan Puritan Movement* (1967).

Remains of Myles Coverdale, Bishop of Exeter, ed. G. Pearson, Parker Society (Cambridge, 1846).

De Lisle, Leanda, *The Sisters Who Would Be Queen: The Tragedy of Mary, Katherine and Lady Jane Grey* (Harper Press, 2010).

Foxe, *The Acts and Monuments of John Foxe*, ed. J. Pratt, vol. v (4th edn; Religious Tract Society, 1877).

Garcia, Ramona, 'Catherine, Duchess of Suffolk' (unpublished dissertation, n.d.).

Goff, Lady Cecilie, *A Woman of the Tudor Age* (John Murray, 1930).

Green, Mary Anne Everett, *Lives of the Princesses of England from the Norman Conquest*, 6 vols (H. Colburn, 1849–55).

Groves, Michael A. R., *Burghley: William Cecil, Lord Burghley* (1998).

Gunn, S. J., *Charles Brandon, Duke of Suffolk, c. 1484–1545* (Wiley-Blackwell, 1988).

Guy, John, *Tudor England* (Oxford, 1988).

Edward Halle, *The Union of the Two Noble and Illustrious Families of Lancaster and York* (1550; reprinted Menston, 1970).

Harkrider, Melissa F., *Women, Reform and Community in Early Modern England: Katherine Willoughby, Duchess of Suffolk, and Lincolnshire's Godly Aristocracy, 1519–1580. Studies in Modern British Religious History* (Boydell, 2008).

Hart, Kelly, *The Mistresses of Henry VIII* (Stroud: The History Press, 2009).

Historical Manuscripts Commission, *Calendar of the Manuscripts of the Marquis of Salisbury preserved at Hatfield House, Hertfordshire*, part 1 (1883), part 2 (1888), part 13 [addenda] (1915).

Historical Manuscripts Commission, *Report on the Manuscripts of the Earl of Ancaster preserved at Grimsthorpe* (1907).

Hogrefe, Pearl, *Women of Action in Tudor England* (Iowa State University Press, 1977).

Howard, Maurice, *The Early Tudor Country House: Architecture and Politics 1490–1550* (1987).

Howard, Maurice, 'Power and the Early Tudor Courtier's House', *History Today* (May 1987).

Ives, Eric, *Lady Jane Grey: A Tudor Mystery* (Wiley-Blackwell, 2011).

Knox, Tim (revised Sally Williams), *Grimsthorpe Castle* (The Grimsthorpe and Drummond Castle Trust, 2003).

Letters and Papers, Foreign and Domestic, of the Reign of Henry VIII 1509–47, ed. J. S. Brewer, J. Gairdner & R. H. Brodie, 21 vols (HMSO, 1862–1910).

Lincolnshire Archives, Ancaster Manuscripts.

Loades, David, *Mary Rose: Tudor Princess, Queen of France. The Extraordinary Life of Henry VIII's Sister* (Stroud: Amberley, 2012).

Machyn, Henry, *The Diary of Henry Machyn A.D. 1550–1563*, ed. J. G. Nichols (Camden Society, 1848).

Martienssen, Anthony, *Queen Katherine Parr* (Cardinal, 1975).

National Archives, State Papers Domestic.

Oxford Dictionary of National Biography, ed. H. C. G. Matthew & B. Harrison, 60 vols (Oxford, 2004). Katherine Bertie by Susan Wabuda; Peregrine Bertie by D. J. B. Trim; Richard Bertie by Susan Wabuda; William Cecil, Lord Burghley by Wallace T. MacCaffrey; Miles Coverdale by David Daniell; John Foxe by Thomas S. Freeman; Stephen Gardiner by C. D. C. Armstrong; Hugh Latimer by Susan Wabuda; Maria Willoughby by Retha M. Warnicke.

Pevsner, Nikolaus, *The Buildings of England: Suffolk* (Harmondsworth, 1961); *Cambridgeshire* (2nd edn, 1970); and John Harris, *Lincolnshire* (1973).

Pettegree, Andrew, *Marian Protestantism: Six Studies* (Aldershot, 1996).

Plowden, Alison, *Lady Jane Grey and the House of Suffolk* (1985).

Porter, Linda, *Katherine the Queen: The Remarkable Life of Katherine Parr* (Pan, 2011).

Read, Evelyn, *Catherine, Duchess of Suffolk: A Portrait* (Cape, 1962).

Rex, Richard, *The Tudors* (Stroud: Amberley, 2011).

Robinson, H. (trans & ed.), *Original Letters Relative to the English Reformation written during the reigns of King Henry VIII, King Edward VI, and Queen Mary, chiefly from the archives of Zurich*, 2 vols (Cambridge, 1846–7).

Sim, Alison, *The Tudor Housewife* (Stroud: Sutton, 1996).

Skidmore, Chris, *Edward VI: The Lost King of England* (Phoenix, 2008).

Thompson, M. W., *Tattershall Castle* (National Trust, 1974).

Tremlett, Giles, *Catherine of Aragon. Henry's Spanish Queen: A Biography* (Faber, 2010).

Wills From Doctors' Commons, ed. J. G. Nichols & J. Bruce (Camden Society, 1863).

Wilson, Derek, *Tudor England* (Shire, 2010).

Wilson, Thomas, *Arte of Rhetorique*, ed. G. H. Mair (Oxford, 1909).

Wright, D. F. (ed.), *Martin Bucer: Reforming Church and Community* (Cambridge, 1994).

Wriothesley, Charles, *A Chronicle of England During the Reigns of the Tudors, from A.D. 1485 to 1559*, ed. W. D. Hamilton, 2 vols (Camden Society, 1875 & 1877).

Zahl, Paul F. M., *Five Women of the English Reformation* (Cambridge, 2001).

LIST OF ILLUSTRATIONS

27. Courtesy of Elizabeth Norton
28. Author's collection
29. Courtesy of Courtesy of Jonathan Reeve JRpc219
30. Author's collection
31. Courtesy of Jonathan Reeve JRCD2b20p961 15501600
32. Courtesy of Nicola Tallis
33. Courtesy of Nicola Tallis
34. Courtesy of Stephen Porter
35. Courtesy of Jonathan Reeve JR1167b4p710 15501600
36. Author's collection
37. Courtesy of the Rijksmuseum
38. Courtesy of Elizabeth Norton
39. Courtesy of Elizabeth Norton
40. Courtesy of Elizabeth Norton
41. Courtesy of Jonathan Reeve JRCD2b20p769
42. Courtesy of Rijksmuseum
43. Author's collection
44. Courtesy of Jonathan Reeve JRCD2b20p1005
45. Courtesy of Shutterstock
46. Courtesy of Shutterstock
47. Courtesy of Nicola Tallis
48. Courtesy of the Rijksmuseum
49. Courtesy of the Yale Center for British Art, Paul Mellon Collection
50. Author's collection
51. Author's collection
52. Courtesy of the Yale Center for British Art, Paul Mellon Collection
53. Author's collection
54. Author's collection
55. Author's collection
56. Author's collection
57. Author's collection
58. Courtesy of Stephen Porter
59. Courtesy of Jonathan Reeve JR735b46fp186 14501500
60. Courtesy of Jonathan Reeve JR992b4p640 14501550
61. Courtesy of Stephen Porter

INDEX

Peers and peeresses are listed under their titles rather than their personal surnames except in a few instances where they are usually known by the latter.